THE
ESSENTIAL
EPICURUS

THE
ESSENTIAL
EPICURUS

LETTERS, PRINCIPAL DOCTRINES,
VATICAN SAYINGS, AND FRAGMENTS

Translated, with an introduction, by
Eugene O'Connor

GREAT BOOKS IN PHILOSOPHY

 **Prometheus Books**

59 John Glenn Drive
Amherst, New York 14228-2119

Published 1993 by Prometheus Books

Inquiries should be addressed to
Prometheus Books
59 John Glenn Drive
Amherst, New York 14228–2119
VOICE: 716–691–0133
FAX: 716–691–0137
WWW.PROMETHEUSBOOKS.COM

14 13 12   12 11 10

Library of Congress Cataloging-in-Publication Data

Epicurus.
    [Selections. English. 1993]
    The essential Epicurus : letters, principal doctrines, Vatican sayings, and fragments / translated, with an introduction, by Eugene O'Connor.
        p. cm. — (Great books in philosophy)
    Includes bibliographical references.
    ISBN 978–0–87975–810–3 (paper)
    1. Philosophy. I. O'Connor, Eugene Michael. II. Title. III. Series.

B570.E5027 1993
187—dc20
                                                    92–42302
                                                    CIP

Printed in the United States of America on acid-free paper

Titles on Metaphysics and Epistemology in Prometheus's Great Books in Philosophy Series

See the back of this volume for a complete list of titles in Prometheus's Great Books in Philosophy and Great Minds series.

Contents

Introduction

EPICURUS, though a citizen of Athens, was born on the island of Samos in 341 B.C. His parents, Neocles and Chaerestrata, were among the 2,000 poor Athenians who had emigrated to Samos in 352 to find economic opportunity. At a very young age, Epicurus began to demonstrate an interest in philosophy and became the student of the Platonist Pamphilus. At eighteen, Epicurus left Samos for Athens to fulfill his compulsory two-year military service as an ephebe, or citizen youth.

The years immediately following the death of Alexander (the Great) were a time of political upheaval. With the expulsion of Athenian colonists from Samos, Epicurus' family moved to Colophon on the Asiatic coast, where Epicurus joined them in 321, at the conclusion of his military service. He lived there for the next ten years, studying under Nausiphanes of Teos. This marked the most crucial period of Epicurus' philosophical training: it was from Nausiphanes that he received instruction in the atomism of Democritus; Epicurus was also influenced by Democritus' concept of "undisturbedness" as the goal of life. But Epicurus would find Democritus too much a determinist, and he would later condemn his teacher Nausiphanes as a "scoundrel and practitioner of such things that cannot lead to wisdom" (*Fragments*, no. 22). In Colophon the Epicurean movement was born. Epicurus' three brothers were among his earliest adherents, and they would remain faithful to him throughout their lives.

In 311, Epicurus left Colophon for Mytilene, a city on the island of Lesbos, where he opened his own school; however, he remained only a short time, having possibly been expelled by the rival Aristotelians. The following year, Epicurus moved to Lampsacus, in Asia Minor, and there won many disciples, including Idomeneus, who provided financial support; Leonteus and his wife Themista; Colotes; Pythocles; and Metrodorus, who would eventually become deputy head of the school.

In 306, Epicurus settled with his students in Athens, which he would make his home until his death. There he purchased a house with a kitchen-garden, thus giving a name to his movement—the Garden. It admitted both men and women, slave and free. Prominent among the students was the courtesan Leontion; we possess a fragment of an affectionate letter Epicurus wrote to her (*Fragments*, no. 32). Epicureanism became not only a philosophy but a way of life. Its adherents were bound by ties of amity: they addressed each other as "friends" and "intimates." The wealthier friends of the school were called upon to give financial support to the others, including Epicurus himself, who, we learn, received a regular stipend (*Fragments*, no. 41). The students of the school were devoted to their master; together they pledged themselves to a life of simple community, withdrawal from politics, and quiet study of the master's world-system. Thus they put into practice the famous Epicurean dictum, *lathe biōsas*, "Live your life without attracting attention," or, more literally, "Live unseen" (*Fragments*, no. 86).

Repudiating Plato's ideal forms, Epicureanism accepted atomism as a valid explanation of the constitution and behavior of matter. Our life is this life on earth, and what we know is what we can perceive through our senses. Based on what we know of earthly phenomena, we can make inferences about the heavenly bodies. By relying on phenomena as self-evidently real, we may discover through our reason what is nonapparent, namely, atoms and void. The universe is eminently material, and that includes the soul of man.

But Epicurus rejected the fatalism of the natural philosophers; he rejected as well the gods of myth. Gods do exist in intervals between worlds in a state of perfect happiness, but they have no concern for men. Punishing and vengeful deities, long the cause of human misery, are misconceptions and, therefore, not real. Human conduct should be motivated not by fear, but by correct reasoning about which actions to pursue and which to avoid. Epicurus' philosophy is thoroughly pragmatic. Take justice, for example: in keeping with his theory of knowledge, which rejects absolutes, Epicurus defines Justice (see *Principal Doctrines*, nos. 36–38) as mutual advantage in men's dealings with each other. And the very notion of justice is variable, changing with altered circumstances.

Epicurus died in 271, at the age of seventy. His chief biographer, the third-century A.D. writer Diogenes Laertius, attributes his death to a stone in the bladder. In one of his letters (*Fragments*, no. 30), Epicurus speaks of the intense pain caused by "strangury and dysentery." A prolific writer, Epicurus left behind over 300 "books" (i.e., papyrus rolls). Among the titles known to us are: *On Nature* (his most important work); *On Atoms and Void; On Love; On Choice and Avoidance; On the Criteria, or the Canon; On Imagery;* and *On the Gods.*

Of Epicurus' vast output we possess but a small portion: three letters to his disciples more or less summarizing the master's cosmological and ethical systems,* and the *Principal Doctrines,* all preserved in Book 10 of Diogenes Laertius' *Lives of the Eminent Philosophers;* brief excerpts and quotations in other ancient writers; and the *Vatican Sayings,* a collection of eighty-one aphorisms discovered in 1888 in a Vatican manuscript. Several of these overlap with the *Principal Doctrines.* We have been helped further by archeological discoveries of fairly recent date. In 1752, carbonized papyrus scrolls of Epicurean texts belonging to the poet and philosopher Philodemus were discovered in the remains of a villa at Herculaneum. French archeologists uncovered in southwestern Turkey, in the year 1884, a lengthy inscription summarizing the Epicurean creed, which had been erected by the millionaire Diogenes Flavianus around A.D. 200.

Epicurus' detractors, both ancient and modern, have been many. Because his school admitted students of both sexes and practiced a life of retirement, the Garden was accused

---

*The style and other features of the letter to Pythocles have long led scholars to suspect that it was not written by Epicurus himself but is a later compilation. However, it contains genuine teachings of the master, and fills in several details of his world-system.

of sponsoring secret orgies. Epicurus himself was maligned as a casuist and a debauchee as well as a charlatan profoundly ignorant of philosophy, whose works were shameless plagiarisms of other authors. Epicurus' ethical theory, which gave prominence to the role of the feelings and the pursuit of pleasure (largely meaning the avoidance of pain), was misconstrued as merely an open invitation to license.

Nonetheless, Epicureanism acquired a devoted following. According to Diogenes Laertius, the philosopher was honored by his country with bronze statues; at the possible risk of hyperbole, Diogenes tells us that Epicurus' friends were so numerous "that they could hardly be counted by entire cities." And the Epicurean school endured after the others had closed (*Lives of the Eminent Philosophers* 10.9–10).

In Rome, Lucretius (ca. 100–55 B.C.) took up the cause of Epicureanism in his great philosophical poem, *On the Nature of the Universe,* which eulogized the founder of the Garden as "our father, the revealer of truth, the giver of fatherly precepts. As bees in flowery glades sip every bloom, so from your pages, O glorious one, we suck the golden maxims, golden, I say, ever worthy of immortal life" (3.9–13, trans. Farrington 1967). Cicero (106–43 B.C.), who himself had little liking for this school of philosophy, has Torquatus describe in the dialogue *De finibus* (1.20.65), how "Epicurus in a single house, and that a small one, maintained a whole company of friends united by the closest sympathy and affection" (trans. Rackham 1914).

The Christians, too, for their part, found elements in the Epicurean world-system which they could appropriate. The early Christian apologist Tertullian (*Apology* 48.11) argued that God created the universe out of opposites: solids and void. And the Christians joined the Epicureans in denouncing pagan superstition.

Medieval Christian praise of Epicurus was meager, however, and reaction to his philosophy mostly negative. In the twelfth century, John of Salisbury, while recognizing the Garden as one of the four schools of antiquity, indicted Epicurus as a crass materialist and sensualist (Letter 187). Dante (*Inferno*, Canto 10.13–15) consigned him to the sixth circle of hell for having denied the immortality of the soul. But the Renaissance saw a rekindling of interest in the teachings of the Garden. In his dialogue *De voluptate* (*On Pleasure*), the Italian humanist Lorenzo Valla (1407–1457) extolled the virtues of Epicureanism, which he regarded rather narrowly as an unshrinking acceptance of sensuality and moral utilitarianism. To the more sober Erasmus (ca. 1466–1536), the Epicureans' devotion to a life of quiet simplicity prefigured Christian asceticism ("Epicureus," 1. 34: *nulli magis sunt Epicurei quam Christiani pie viventes*). The essayist Michel de Montaigne (1533–1592) and the philosopher Giordano Bruno (*Degli Eroici Furori*, 1585) championed Epicurus' doctrine of pleasure and especially his revolt against those fake religions that deny any significance to this earthly life, proclaiming instead some vaguely conceived existence after death.

It was in the seventeenth century, however, with the French philosopher Pierre Gassendi (1592–1655), that Epicureanism enjoyed a true revival and once more earned its rightful place as a serious philosophy for an increasingly secular world. Gassendi's *Eight Books on the Life and Manners of Epicurus*, published in 1647, enjoyed great success in England, where it influenced Thomas Hobbes; John Locke; Walter Charleton, author of *Epicurus' Morals;* and the great man of letters Sir William Temple, who wrote *Upon the Garden of Epicurus, or Of Gardening* (1685). Early in the next century, John Digby's edition of Epicurus (1712), though it misrepresents much of the master's teaching, also did its part to rescue him from long neglect. In the nineteenth century, Epicureanism's influence can be seen in the materialism of Karl Marx; recent scholarship (e.g., Mitsis 1988) has drawn comparisons between Epicurus' ethical system and the utilitarianism of John Stuart Mill.

The extant writings of Epicurus are fragmentary and often obscure, although the scholia help throw light on some dark passages. For my translation I have used the editions of Usener (1887), von der Muehll (1922), and Bailey (1926, 1975). Usener's edition, while still the basic sourcebook of Greek and Latin texts bearing on Epicurus, was published too soon to contain the *Vatican Sayings,* which do appear in von der Muehll. Bailey, although a smaller collection than Usener, includes the *Vatican Sayings* as well as fragments from the Herculanean papyri and from the inscription of Diogenes Flavianus not found in Usener. The ordering of my own text, for the most part, follows Bailey.

Eugene O'Connor

References and Bibliography

Asmis, Elizabeth. *Epicurus' Scientific Method.* Ithaca and London: Cornell University Press, 1984.

Bailey, Cyril, ed., trans., and comm. *Epicurus: The Extant Remains.* Oxford: Clarendon Press, 1926. Reprint. Hildesheim: Georg Olms Verlag, 1975.

———. *The Greek Atomists and Epicurus.* Oxford: Clarendon Press, 1928.

Brunschwig, Jacques, and Martha C. Nussbaum, eds. *Passions and Perceptions: Studies in Hellenistic Philosophy of Mind.* New York: Cambridge University Press, 1993.

DeLacy, P. H. "Epicurus." *The Encyclopedia of Philosophy.* Vol. 3. New York: Macmillan Publishing Co., Inc., and The Free Press, 1972.

De Witt, N. W. *Epicurus and His Philosophy.* Minneapolis, Minn.: University of Minnesota Press, 1954. Reprint. Westport, Conn.: Greenwood Press, 1973.

Digby, John, trans. and comm. *The Life and Morals of Epicurus.* London, 1712.

Erasmus, Desiderius. "Epicureus." Vol. 3 of *Opera Omnia Desiderii Erasmi Rotterodami,* edited by L.-E. Halkin, F. Bierlaire, and R. Hoven. Amsterdam: North-Holland Publishing Company, 1972.

Farrington, Benjamin. *The Faith of Epicurus.* New York: Basic Books, 1967.

Festugière, A. J. *Epicurus and His Gods.* Trans. C. W. Chilton. Oxford: Blackwell, 1955.

Hibler, Richard W. *Happiness through Tranquility: The School of Epicurus.* New York and London: University Press of America, 1984.

Jones, Howard. *The Epicurean Tradition.* London and New York: Routledge, 1989.

Millor, W. J., S.J., and C. N. L. Brooke, eds. *The Letters of John of Salisbury.* 2 vols. Oxford: Clarendon Press, 1979.

Mitsis, Philip. *Epicurus' Ethical Theory: The Pleasures of Invulnerability.* Ithaca and London: Cornell University Press, 1988.

Osler, Margaret, ed. *Atoms, Pneuma, and Tranquillity: Epicurean and Stoic Themes in European Thought.* New York: Cambridge University Press, 1991.

Rackham, H., trans. *Cicero, De finibus bonorum et malorum.* Cambridge, Mass.: Harvard University Press, 1914.

Rist, J. M. *Epicurus: An Introduction.* Cambridge: Cambridge University Press, 1972.

Strodach, George K. *The Philosophy of Epicurus.* Evanston, Ill.: Northwestern University Press, 1963.

von der Muehll, P., ed. *Epicuri epistulae tres et ratae sententiae.* Stuttgart: Teubner, 1922.

Usener, H., ed. *Epicurea.* Leipzig: Teubner, 1887.

Wilbur, J. B., and H. J. Allen, eds. *The Worlds of the Early Greek Philosophers.* Buffalo, N.Y.: Prometheus Books, 1979.

Letter to Herodotus*

INTRODUCTION

For those who are unable, Herodotus, to investigate care- 35†
fully each of my books on nature or to peruse any lengthier
compositions, I have prepared an epitome, or summary,‡
of the entire system for them to retain at least a general
outline of my ideas, so that, as the occasion arises, they
may be able to rely on themselves in the chief parts, inso-
far as they take up the study of nature. But even those
who have made considerable advancement in their inquiry

---

*The Herodotus addressed here is a follower of Epicurus who
later became disenchanted with the master and began publishing
scurrilous attacks against Epicurus which impugned his Athenian
citizenship (see Diogenes Laertius, *Lives of the Eminent Philosophers*
10.4).

†The reason why the section numbers begin at 35 is that this
letter follows sections 1-34 in Book 10 of Diogenes Laertius, the "life"
of Epicurus.

‡This is known as the Greater Epitome, which set out the main
principles of Epicurus' teachings in different areas. This letter, by
contrast, is known as the Lesser Epitome.

into my complete works should keep in mind the model of the entire treatise which has been reduced to its elements. For while we frequently need the entire conception, 36 we do not in like manner need it in all its particulars. Indeed, we must return to those principal points and constantly recall to mind just enough to give us the overall outline of the facts. To be sure, when the principal points have been well grasped and remembered, exact knowledge in all its details will be discovered; for the most important feature of all exact knowledge, even for one fully initiated, is the ability to make swift use of direct apprehension and knowledge summarized in simple principles and formulae. For compression of the course of study of the system as a whole is impossible if one cannot comprehend in brief formulae everything that may also be ob- 37 served accurately in every detail. Therefore, since there is available such a useful avenue for those who have become familiar with the study of nature, I, who recommend constant activity in natural science and who am most at peace in living this sort of life, have composed for you such an epitome and outline of all my teachings.

Rules of Procedure

First of all, Herodotus, we must comprehend the meanings that underlie the words, so that, by referring to them, we may be able to reach judgments concerning opinions, matters of inquiry, or problems and not leave everything undecided as we argue endlessly or use words that have 38 no sense. Therefore, it is necessary that the first concept answering to the word be clear and in no need of explanation, if we shall have a standard for referring to the inquiry, the problem, or the opinion. Furthermore, we must maintain all our investigations in accordance with our sensations and especially our ready application whether of mind or of any one of our means of judging, and likewise in accordance with our feelings. In this way, we shall have the means by which we may judge both the problem of sense perception and the nonapparent.

THE UNIVERSE AND ITS CONSTITUENT ELEMENTS

Having made this distinction, we must now consider what is not evident to our senses: first of all, that nothing is created from what does not exist. For everything would be born from everything without the need for seed. And 39 if that which is destroyed were dissolved into what does not exist, everything would be destroyed, since that into which they were dissolved does not exist. Moreover, the universe was and always will be the same as it is now. For there is nothing into which it changes. Beyond the universe there is nothing which, entering into it, could accomplish the change.

Bodies and Void

Furthermore, the universe consists of bodies and void: that bodies exist, perception itself in all men bears witness; it is through the senses that we must by necessity form a judgment about the imperceptible by means of reason,

40 just as I argued above. But if that which we call void and
place and impalpable substance did not exist, bodies would
have no place to be nor anything through which to move,
as they are clearly seen to be moving. Beyond this, nothing can even be thought of, either by the understanding
or on analogy with things comprehensible, as are grasp-
able as entire substances and not spoken of as attributes
or accidents of them. And of the bodies some are compounds and others are those from which the compounds
41 have been formed: these latter are indivisible and un-
changeable if everything is not about to be reduced to
nonexistence; but some strong element remains in the
breakup of the compounds, one that is solid by nature
and incapable of being dissolved. As a result, the first
beginnings must be indivisible bodily substances.

The Infinity of the Universe

Furthermore, the universe is without limit. For that which
is limited has an outermost edge; the outermost edge will
be seen against something else. As a result, the universe,
having no outermost edge, has no limit; having no limit
it would be boundless and unlimited. Also, the universe
is boundless both in the number of the bodies and the
42 magnitude of the void. If the void were limitless and the
bodies limited, the bodies would not remain anywhere,
but be borne and scattered into the limitless void, having nothing to support them and check them by colliding
with them. But if the void were limited, there would not
be enough room in it for a limitless number of bodies.
    In addition, the indivisible and solid bodies from which

compound substances are created and into which they are dissolved are incomprehensible in the varieties of their shapes; for it is impossible that such varieties arise from the same shapes if they are limited in number. In each configuration the number of atoms is infinite; but in their varieties they are not absolutely infinite but only incomprehensible.

Atoms' Motion

The atoms move continuously forever, some . . .* stand-   43
ing at a long distance from one another, others in turn maintaining their rapid vibration, whenever they happen to be checked by their interlacing with others or covered by the interlaced atoms. It is both the nature of the void   44
separating each atom by itself that effects this, since it is unable to furnish any resistance, and the hardness belonging to the atoms that makes them rebound after colliding, to the extent that their interlacing grants them a return to their former position following collision. Of their motions there is no beginning; the atoms and the void are the cause.

    This discourse thus far, keeping all these points in   45
mind, provides a sufficient outline for the understanding of existing things.

The Infinite Number of Worlds

Moreover, there are infinite worlds, both like and unlike this one. For the atoms, being endless, as has just been demonstrated, are borne over a very great distance. For

---

*There is a gap in the text here.

these atoms, out of which a world might be born and by which it might be made, have not been used up for the creation either of a single world or of a limited number, nor of however many worlds are alike or however many are different from these. Therefore, there is no impediment to the infinitude of worlds.

Sense Perception

46a Furthermore, there are images having the same shape as the solid objects, but far removed from objects apparent to the senses owing to their subtlety. For it is not impossible that such emanations arise in the air surrounding the objects, nor that there arise tendencies toward the manufacture of hollow spaces and subtleties, nor that such emanations maintain the constant position and order they had in the solid bodies. We call these images films that are given off by the object and that convey an impression to the eyes.

47a   Next, nothing in the objects apparent to the senses invalidates the assertion that the films, or emanations, have unsurpassable fineness and subtlety. Hence they also have unsurpassable speed since their passage is completely uniform, owing to the fact that little or nothing of them collides with the infinite atoms, while bodies composed of

48 many or infinite atoms immediately collide with something. In addition, nothing refutes the assertion that the films or emanations occur with the speed of thought. For their flow from the surface of bodies is constant, though not evident by any diminution of the body owing to the constant filling up of atoms; so the flowing preserves for a long time the position and arrangement of atoms in the solid

body—even if it is sometimes muddled—and combinations
are quickly formed in the surrounding atmosphere because
there is no need for their substance to be filled in deep
inside. And there are some other ways by which such emanations are produced. None of what I have said is contradicted
by the senses, if we regard in what way they will bring
clear visions from the world outside and the relations between external objects.

We must also consider that when something of exter- 49
nal objects enters into us, we see and have in mind its
shape. For external things could not impress on us the
nature of their color and size by means of the air lying
between us and them, nor by means of rays or by some
sort of current that flows from us to them, in the same
way as when certain models emanating from the things
themselves and having the same color and shape enter in
the appropriate size into our sight and mind. Since they 50
move quickly, they give the illusion of a single continuous
motion, and they preserve as well the relationship with the
existing object, as a result of the measured contact with
that body owing to the rapid movement of atoms deep
inside the solid object. And whatever image we receive by
direct apprehension of our mind or our sense organs, whether
of shape or of essential properties, that is the true shape
of the solid object, since it is created by the constant repeti-
tion of the image or the impression it has left behind.

There is always falsehood and error involved in im-
porting into judgment an element additional to sense impressions, either to confirm or deny.* For there would be 51

---

*The text is uncertain here.

no correspondence between the images that are received
as in a picture, or those arising in dreams or as a result
of application by the mind or the other faculties, and things
that exist and are called real, unless there were such efflu-
ences actually brought into contact with our senses. There
would be no error, unless there occurred within us some
other movement connected with the perception of images
but distinguished from it. It is from this, if it is not confirmed or is contradicted by evidence, that error results;
52   but truth, if it is confirmed or not contradicted. We must
by all means keep this in mind, so that neither the standards of judgment that result from perceptions may be
confuted nor error that has thoroughly established itself
as truth likewise throw everything into confusion.

Hearing

Moreover, hearing results from a certain current or flow
being carried from the one speaking or what is sounding
or making a noise, or giving rise in such manner to a
sensation of hearing. This current is divided into particles,
each like the other, which preserve at the same time a
certain affinity with each other and a distinctive unity which
extends as far back as what produced the sound. This unity
commonly produces perception in the recipient, or at least
53   furnishes clear evidence of an external object. Without this
affinity or correspondence arising from the object, there
would be no such perception. We must not think that the
air itself is being shaped by the emission of a voice or
similar sounds—for the air will be very far from being
so affected—but that whenever we emit the sound of speech,

the impact that occurs within us produces a squeezing out of certain particles that emit a stream, or current, of sound, and this furnishes us with the sensation of hearing.

Smell

Moreover, we must consider that the sense of smell, like hearing, would never produce a sensation, unless there were certain particles of suitable size that are borne from the object to arouse this organ of sense, some of them confusedly and unpleasantly, others calmly and agreeably.

THE ATOMS

And, furthermore, we must consider that atoms exhibit   54
none of the qualities belonging to visible things except shape, mass, and size, and whatever is necessarily related to shape. For every quality changes; but the atoms do not change, since, in the dissolution of compound substances, there must remain something solid and indestructible, which causes changes not into the nonexistent, nor from the nonexistent, but as a result of the transpositions of some particles and the approach or departure of others. Therefore, it is necessary that these shifting particles be everlasting and not share in the nature of what is changeable, but rather possess their own mass and configurations. For they must needs remain permanent. Even among things perceptible to us   55
that change their configurations by loss of matter, there is still perceived an inherent shape; the other qualities do not remain in the object as it changes, just as shape survives,

but they are removed from the entire body. These properties that are left behind are enough to cause the differences in compound substances, since it is necessary that some at least remain and are not destroyed into the nonexistent.

Moreover, we must not think that every size exists in atoms, lest visible phenomena offer contrary evidence; yet we must think that there are certain differences in size. For if this is so, we shall give a better account of things 56 that arise through the feelings and sensations. The existence of every size is not necessary to explain the differences in qualities; at the same time, if atoms were of every size, some atoms would necessarily be visible to us. But this is not the case, nor is it possible to conceive how an atom might become visible.*

The Parts of the Atom

In addition to this, we must not think that in a limited body there is an infinite number of particles no matter how small. Therefore, we must not only reject a cutting into ever smaller parts to infinity, lest we deprive all things of strength and in the composition of aggregate bodies be compelled to consume existing things by reducing them to nonexistence; but we must also not think that in finite bodies a reduction to ever smaller parts to infinity can 57 occur. For if once someone asserts that in anything there are infinite parts or parts of any degree of smallness, it is impossible to conceive how this object could still be limited in size. For it is clear that the infinite particles must

---

*Epicurus is probably arguing here against Democritus, who accepted the existence of very large atoms (see Jones 1989: 31).

be of such-and-such a size; and however small they be, the size of the body, too, would be infinite. And since the limited body has an outermost point that can be distinguished, even if it is not visible by itself, it is impossible to think that the adjacent point is not of the same kind, and that thus it happens that if one were to proceed forward in his mind to the next point in line, he would continue to mark such points to infinity.

We must also understand that the least element in sensation is neither wholly what allows us to progress from part to part nor wholly unlike it; although it bears something in common with divisible bodies, it cannot be divided into parts. But whenever, as a result of this resemblance or similarity, we think to mark off a portion of it on this side or that, it must happen that another part like the preceding comes into our view. If we look at these points in succession, beginning with the first and not lingering on the same point, we find that they do not touch each other, part to part, but rather measure their size within the compass of their own individual characteristics, the greater body measuring more and the smaller body fewer. We must also imagine that the smallest element in the atom makes use of this same relation of part to whole. For while it clearly differs from what is visible owing to its small size, it still makes use of this same proportion. We have stated that the atom has size, on the basis of its relation to perceptible bodies, although we regard the atom as inferior because of its smallness. Furthermore, in our mental perception regarding invisible bodies, we must consider these smallest uncompounded parts of the atom as boundaries, providing in themselves the primary measure of size or

58

59

magnitude for the larger and smaller atoms. For the common element they share with the unchanging parts of sensible things is sufficient to justify our conclusion to this extent; but it is impossible for there to be a coming together of the least parts of atoms as bodies that are in motion.

60   Furthermore, regarding the infinite, we do not say "up" or "down" as though with reference to a topmost or bottommost point. Although it is possible to proceed to infinity starting from the point above our heads where we are standing, this absolute highest point will never be visible to us. Nor can what lies beneath the point thought of to infinity be up and down at the same time with regard to the same thing. For this is impossible to conceive. Thus we may assume a single motion that is thought of as proceeding upward to infinity and a single motion in a downward direction, even if what passes from us in the direction of the spaces above our heads arrives countless times at the feet of those above us, and what is borne from us in a downward direction reaches the heads of those below. For nonetheless one of the motions is thought of as extending in one direction to infinity, the other extending in the opposite direction.

61   Furthermore, the atoms must possess equal velocity, whenever they move through the void, with nothing coming into collision with them. For neither will heavy bodies move more swiftly than the small and light, when nothing encounters them; nor do the small bodies move more quickly than the large, since they maintain a uniform course, provided nothing collides with them. Nor is the motion upward or sideways owing to collision swifter, nor the motion downward owing to its weight. For to the

extent that either motion is maintained, so long will it keep on a course as swift as thought, until something collides with it, either from outside or from its own weight, which counteracts the force of what struck it.

Moreover, the atoms' passage through the void, when 46b it meets no object that collides with them, completes any conceivable distance in an inconceivably brief time. For collision, or the absence of it, assumes the likeness of slowness or speed.

Furthermore, in compound substances one atom will 62 be said to be swifter than another, although the atoms are of equal velocity, because even in the least period of continuous time, the atoms are moving in clusters toward one place. However, in a passage of time perceptible only to the mind, they move not in one direction, but are constantly colliding with one another until the constancy of their motion comes under scrutiny of the senses. What opinion adds to sense impressions regarding the invisible, namely, that the moments perceptible only by thought will have continuity of motion, is not true in this case, for only what is perceived by the senses or grasped by mental apprehension is true.

Nor must we suppose that in moments perceptible 47b only to thought the entire moving compound also moves in several directions, for this is inconceivable. If this were so, when it arrived all together in a perceptible period of time from any quarter of the infinite, it would not have set out from the place from which we perceived its motion. This visible motion will be the result of internal collision even if up to the visible level we admit that the speed of its motion meets no resistance from collision. It is useful also to grasp this fundamental principle.

THE SOUL

Its Composition

63 Next you must, referring to the perceptions and the feelings—for in these there will lie the most reliable certainty—consider that the soul is a body of fine particles dispersed throughout the entire organism and most resembling a wind that contains a certain mixture of heat, in some ways resembling this (the wind) and in others this (the heat). And there is a part of the soul that is very different even from these in subtlety of composition and is therefore more interactive, or more in sympathy, with the rest of the organism. All this is made evident by the powers of the mind, its feelings, its mobility, and those faculties of which we are deprived when we die.

The Soul and Sensation

Furthermore, you must understand that the soul is the
64 chief cause of sensation. But it would not have acquired this faculty, if it were not somehow enclosed by the rest of the body.

The rest of the body, having provided to the soul this cause of sensation, has itself acquired from the soul a share in this capacity, although not all the sensations that the soul has acquired. For this reason, the body has no sensation once the soul departs. For the body did not acquire this power on its own, but made it possible for the companion being that came into existence at the same time. This other being, through the power immediately brought

to perfection within itself as a result of motion, imparted
to the body the faculty of sensation resulting from its
juxtaposition and affinity with the body, as I have said.
Therefore, the soul, so long as it remains within the body,   65
will never cease to feel sensation even when some other
part of the body is lost. If part of the soul be destroyed
with its enclosure, when that enclosure is wholly or par-
tially destroyed—if the soul remains at all, it will have sensation. But the rest of the body, even if it abides in whole
or in part, will not have sensation when that aggregate
of atoms, of whatever size, that goes to produce the nature of soul, is missing. Moreover, if the entire body is
destroyed, the soul disperses and no longer possesses the
same faculties, nor does it move, so that as a result it does
not possess sensation.

It is not possible to imagine the soul existing and hav-   66
ing sensation without the body, and experiencing these
movements when there no longer exists that which encloses
and surrounds the soul, in which it now exists and has
these movements.

The Material Nature of the Soul

We must, in addition, note that the word "incorporeal" is   67
most commonly applied to what may be thought of as
existing by itself. It is impossible to imagine the incorporeal as an independent existence except as the void. The
void can neither act nor be acted upon, but only furnishes
to bodies motion through it. For this reason, those who
claim that the soul is incorporeal are talking rubbish, for
the soul would not be able to act or be acted upon if that

were so. But as the case stands, both these occurrences are
68   clearly distinguished in connection with the soul. Therefore,
anyone who refers all these considerations concerning the
soul to his feelings and sensations, remembering what was
said at the beginning, will observe that they are comprehended by these general principles in a manner sufficient
to enable him to work out the details for himself with
certainty, starting from these general formulae.

PROPERTIES AND ACCIDENTS

Properties

Furthermore, regarding shapes, colors, mass, weight, and
whatever else is predicated of the body, as if they were
essential properties of all things or those things visible to
and knowable by the perceptions, we must not consider
them as independent existences (for this is impossible to
69   conceive), nor as wholly without existence, nor as certain
other incorporeal elements existing beside the body, nor
as portions of it; rather, we must suppose that the body
owes its own permanent existence to all of them. Yet the
body cannot exist as an assemblage of parts brought together to form it (as when a greater structure is assembled
from its constituent parts, whether primary elements or
parts smaller than the whole, whatever it is), but only as
it has its own permanent character as a result of all these
properties. These properties all exist with their own peculiar
distinctions, provided the aggregate structure or body at-
tends them and is in no sense torn from them, but instead

has assumed the predicate of body by virtue of its aggregate comprehension of the properties.

Accidents

Moreover, it often happens to bodies that accidents that   70
are neither incorporeal nor in the class of invisible things
accompany them, but not permanently.* As a result, when
we employ this term "accidents" according to the most
general usage, we make it clear that they possess neither
the nature of the whole, which we call "body," understanding it in its aggregate sense, nor the nature of the properties that constantly attend it, without which a body cannot
be conceived. They might each be called by this name as   71
a result of certain acts of apprehension when the aggregate
body accompanies them, but only whenever each is seen
to be occurring, since accidents are not constant accompaniments. There is no expelling this distinct perception
(about accidents) from the realm of being, because they
do not possess the nature of the whole (called "body")
to which they are attached, nor that of the properties that
are in permanent attendance. We are not to think of these
accidents as existing independently—for this cannot be
conceived in the case either of accidents or permanent
accompaniments—but all accidents are to be regarded as
they appear to be: neither attending permanently nor possessing the status of material substance; rather, they are
seen in the manner in which the actual act of perception
reveals their proper characteristics.

---

*Bailey marks a lacuna here; von der Muehll brackets the line
as corrupt.

Time

72 Moreover, we are to firmly grasp this additional point as well. We must not search for time as we do for the other things that we look for in an object, referring to the images we have in our minds, but must draw from direct experience, according to which we speak of "a long time" or "a short time," applying our intuition to this as we do to other things.* And we must not adopt new expressions as preferable, but use those already in existence for it. Nor must we predicate of time anything else as having the same existence as this unique property (for certain people do do this), but take into consideration only that with which
73 we associate time and by which we measure it. For this stands in need not of demonstration but only of reflection on the fact that we associate time with days and nights and portions of them, just as we do with feelings and lack of feeling, motion and rest, recognizing time as a certain particular sort of accident of these things, by virtue of which we call it time.

THE WORLDS

In addition to what has already been said, we must believe that the world and every limited compound that constantly presents a likeness in appearance to the things we see

---

*I.e., just as in other cases we use the immediate data of sense to determine the nature of the thing perceived, so we must use our direct intuition to determine the nature of time. . . ." (Bailey's note *ad loc.*)

have been created from the infinite, all of them, greater and lesser, separated off from individual physical masses; and that all are again dissolved, some more quickly, others more slowly, some suffering from one set of conditions, others from a different set. It is clear that . . . * Further- 74 more, we must not think that worlds were created of necessity with only one shape . . .†, for no one could prove that in a world of one sort there might or might not have been included the kinds of seeds from which living creatures, plants, and all the rest of visible nature take shape, and that in another world this could not have happened.

THE RISE OF CIVILIZATION

The Development of the Arts and of Language

Moreover, we must assume that human beings have been 75 taught and constrained in many and manifold ways by circumstances; and that reason later worked out in detail what had been suggested by nature and made new discoveries, in some areas quickly, in others more slowly. In certain

---

*The text is lacunose here. The scholiast inserts the following note to this passage: "Likewise, in the work titled *On Nature* he [Epicurus] says that the worlds are perishable, with parts being exchanged one for the other. And elsewhere, that the earth floats upon the air."

†There follows another gap in the text. Again, says the scholiast: "The differences are those he [Epicurus] recounts in Book 12 of his work *On Nature*. Some worlds are spherical, others egg-shaped, and still others of varying shape. They do not, however, have any shape; nor can living things exist if separated from the infinite." Epicurus takes up this problem again in the letter to Pythocles, sec. 88.

periods men made greater progress; in others, less. Therefore, names were not assigned in the beginning by arbitrary decree, but rather the natures of humankind, as they felt their own peculiar feelings according to their different nationalities and received their own peculiar sense perceptions, each in their own way emitted air (i.e., uttered a sound) given form by their particular feelings and impressions, according to the 76 difference in nations owing to their various locations. Later, specific vocal sounds were agreed upon by mutual consent in the individual nations in order that the meanings of what was said might be less ambiguous and clarified more concisely. And items still unfamiliar were brought in by people who already knew about them and recommended sounds for these things. Sometimes they were constrained to utter brand-new sounds; at other times, they chose by logical selection, in conformance with prevailing usage, what word they would use to make their meaning clear.

THE HEAVENLY PHENOMENA

Their Causes

Furthermore, we must not suppose that the motions of heavenly bodies, their turning and eclipses, risings and settings, and related actions are the result of some being who arranges or has ordained them and at the same time en- 77 joys every blessedness along with immortality. For troubles and cares, anger and good will, do not accord with blessedness, but rather arise in weakness, fear, and need for one's neighbors close by.

Nor must we think that fire that has been formed into a mass has acquired blessedness and undertaken all these motions of its own free will. But we must preserve, in every term that applies to such concepts of blessedness, this majesty in its entirety, so that there may not grow out of them opinions that are incongruous with this idea of majesty. If we do not do this, this very incongruity will result in the greatest turmoil in our souls. Therefore, we must believe that it is as a result of the original inclusion of these physical masses in the birth of the world that this law governing their orbits was also ordained.

The Study of the Heavenly Phenomena

Moreover, we must believe that it is the task of natural   78
science to work out in detail the causes of the most im- portant facts; and that happiness in the knowledge about the celestial phenomena lies in this, and in the understand- ing of the phenomena visible in the heavens, and of what- ever else is proper to accurate knowledge for this end (be- ing happiness). Further, we must not think that in such mat- ters there is anything that admits of variation of random- ness; absolutely nothing in an immortal and blessed nature may suggest dispute or disturbance. That this is absolutely so, it is possible for us to ascertain by our intelligence.

What falls within the inquiry concerning settings,   79
risings, revolutions, and eclipses, and whatever is related to these, no longer has relevance to the happiness resulting from knowledge; those who, although they have learned these things, are yet ignorant of the original nature and the essential causes, remain fearful, as if they knew noth-

ing at all. Their fears may increase, when the wonder arising from the perception of these phenomena is unable to
provide a solution to the problem of their relation to the
essential principles. Therefore, even if we shall discover
several causes for revolutions, risings, settings, eclipses, and
things of this kind, just as it was in the case of particular
80   details, we must not think that our investigation into these
matters has not reached a level sufficient to lead to our
happiness and peace of mind. Therefore, keeping in mind
how many ways a similar phenomenon occurs on earth,
we must inquire into the causes of the heavenly phenomena and all that is not clearly evident to the senses. We
must also pay no attention to those who fail to distinguish
what exists or comes into being in one way only from
what occurs in several ways, as in the case of those phenomena that can be seen only from a distance; and who,
furthermore, do not know under what circumstances it is
impossible to achieve peace of mind. Therefore, if we think
that a phenomenon comes into being in some particular
way and likewise under conditions in which it is possible to enjoy peace of mind, when we know that it can
happen in many ways, we shall remain just as undisturbed
as if we knew that the phenomenon occurred in some
particular manner.

The Chief Causes of Humankind's Fears

81   In addition to all this we must understand this further
point, that the chief disturbance in the minds of humankind arises when they think that these heavenly bodies
are blessed and immortal but have at the same time wills,

actions, and motives that are opposed to these divine attributes; and when they are constantly expecting and fearing some everlasting pain, as happens in myths. Or they fear the loss of sensation itself that comes with death, as if it were something that affected them directly. Human beings are put in this state not by correct judgment but by some irrational impulse. Therefore, since they cannot define or set a limit to the marvelous and strange, they suffer an equally or even more intense disturbance than if they had applied a rational judgment to these matters. 82 But peace of mind means being released from all this and retaining constantly in memory the general and most important principles.

Therefore, we must be attentive to the feelings that we have and to sensations both common and particular in accordance with a common or particular concern, as well as to every available perception, according to each of the standards of judgment. For if we attend to these, we shall correctly reckon the causes from which disturbance and fear arise and, tracing the causes of the heavenly bodies and the remaining phenomena that occasionally occur, we shall be rid of whatever is utterly terrifying to the rest of humankind.

CONCLUSION

This, Herodotus, is my treatise for you on the whole of 83 nature, abridged so that this account may be capable of being grasped with precision. I think that, even if a person cannot proceed to each of the investigations in detail, he will obtain from this a strength far superior to that of other men. Indeed, he will clarify on his own many of the detailed investigations in reference to our entire treatise, and these very principles stored up in his memory will aid him constantly. For they are such that even those who have made considerable progress, or even achieved mastery, in working out the individual details will complete the greater part of their studies of the whole of nature in accordance with such principles as I have laid down. And as for those not fully in the company of the ones perfecting themselves—of them there are those who, without verbal instruction, can hastily survey the principal points with a view to achieving tranquility.

Letter to Pythocles[*]

INTRODUCTION

Cleon brought me a letter from you, in which you continue 84
to show your kindness toward me in a manner worthy of
my feelings toward you; and in which you attempt, not without some degree of conviction, to recall the arguments which
lead to a happy life. You ask me to send you a brief and
concise discussion about the heavenly bodies, so that you may
easily recall it; for you say that what I have written in my
other works is difficult to remember, although you have them
constantly to hand. I received your request with pleasure and
felt compelled to reply with agreeable expectations for the future. Therefore, having completed all my other writing, I shall 85
fulfill your request. These arguments will be useful as well
to many others, especially to those who have newly tasted
the genuine teachings about nature and those too deeply involved in the business of everyday life. Therefore, grasp it
well and, keeping it in memory, proceed to study it diligently
along with what else I sent in the Lesser Epitome to Herodotus.

---

[*]Pythocles is a youth who joined Epicurus' school at Mytilene.

The Reason for Study

First of all, we must not think that there is any other aim
of knowledge about the heavens, whether treated in
connection with other doctrines or separately, than peace
of mind and unshakeable confidence, just as it is our aim
86   in all other pursuits. We must not force impossible explanations nor conduct the same mode of investigation in
everything as we do in matters of how to live or in clari-
fication of other physical problems, such as: "The universe
consists of bodies and the impalpable," or "The elements
are indivisible," and everything that has but a single explanation agreeing with observed facts. This is not the case
with the heavenly bodies; rather, they have more than a
single cause of their creation and more than a single explanation for their existence which harmonizes with our
senses. For we must not theorize scientifically about nature by means of empty maxims and arbitrary principles,
87   but as phenomena require. For our life has no need of
foolishness and idle opinion, but of an existence free from
confusion. Everything occurs without disturbance in accordance with what admits a variety of explanations that
are in accordance with observed phenomena, whenever we
admit—as we must—a probable explanation for them; but
whenever we admit one explanation but reject another that
agrees equally well with the evidence, it is clear that we
fall short in every way of true scientific inquiry and resort
instead to myth. It is possible to receive certain indica-
tions from visible signs here on earth about what goes on
in the heavens, although we cannot observe the heavenly
phenomena directly. For these signs may be produced in

a variety of ways. Yet the appearance of each heavenly   88
phenomenon must be carefully observed and, as regards
the things associated with it, those events which offer
evidence that they are occurring in a number of ways not
incompatible with our earthly experience, must be carefully distinguished.

WORLDS

Definitions

A world is a circumscribed portion of sky, embracing heavenly bodies, earth, and all encompassing phenomena. If it
is destroyed, everything contained in it will be confounded.
It is separated from the boundless and is limited by a
boundary either loose or compact, either revolving or sta-
tionary, and possessing a shape that is spherical or three-
cornered or any kind at all. All sorts of variations are possible, for none of the phenomena in this world, whose
boundary it is possible to comprehend, offers evidence to
the contrary.

We may assume that such worlds are limitless in num-   89
ber, and that such a world is able to be born inside a
world and in an interworld, by which we mean an interval between worlds. This happens in a place mostly empty
—but not in a large place that is absolutely empty, as
some say—when suitable seeds flow together from a single world or interval between two worlds, or else from
several worlds. These gradually form attachments and
come together, and shift their position to another place,

90 if this so occurs, and suitable matter flows in until the world is made complete and permanent, as long as the underlying foundations can receive additional matter. For it is not merely necessary that condensation or a whirl occur by constraint in the empty space in which a world is to be born, according to some; nor can a world grow until it knocks against another world, as one of the so-called physical philosophers says.* For that is contradicted by phenomena.

The Heavenly Bodies

91 The sun, the moon, and the other stars did not come into being on their own to be later encompassed by the world, but they were molded straightaway, and began to increase in size by accretions and whirlings of certain bodies of fine parts, either of wind or of fire or of both; our senses suggest that this is so. To us, the size of the sun, moon, and stars is as great as it appears to be. The actual size is greater than what we see or slightly smaller or the same. Just so do fires on earth, when seen from a distance, appear to the senses. And every objection at this point will be easily resolved, if we apply our attention to the clear view, as I demonstrate in my books on nature.

Their Risings and Settings

92 The risings and settings of the sun, the moon, and the other stars may happen as a result of kindling and being

---

*Another probable reference to Democritus. See Bailey's note *ad loc.*

quenched, with the surrounding spaces in the regions where
they rise and set being such that these results will occur;
nothing in the phenomena offers evidence to contradict
this. These effects may also be brought about by their
appearance above the earth or, in turn, by the earth moving in front of them. This, too, is in agreement with the
evidence. It is not impossible that their movements occur
as the result of the revolution of the entire sky; or else
the sky does not move, but the heavenly bodies revolve
as the result of a natural impulse toward the site of their
rising, which was produced at the beginning of the
world . . .* by a heat as the result of a certain spreading   93
of fire, which always moves regularly toward one place,
then another. It is possible that the tropics of the sun and
moon† are the result of the obliquity of the sky as it is
constrained by the changing seasons; equally possible that
these events result from a counterthrust of air or appropriate matter constantly being set on fire, as other matter
fails. Or this revolving motion may have been assigned
to these heavenly bodies from the beginning, so that they
move in a kind of spiral. For all these and related observations are not at variance with what is manifestly visible, if in such considerations as these we keep hold of what
is possible and have the ability to refer each of these points
to what accords with the evidence, without being afraid
of the servile artifices of the astronomers.

---

*There is a gap in the text here.

†See Bailey's note *ad loc.*: "Besides appearing to perform a
revolution, they [the sun and moon] seem also to go up and down
in the sky, standing higher in the heavens at one part of their orbit
than another."

94   The waning of the moon and its subsequent waxing could be due to the rotation of this body itself and likewise to the configurations of the air, or yet again to interpositions of bodies, or any of the ways which phenomena in our own experience offer as explanations of what is seen in the moon. Only let us not become content with the method of the single clause and reject all the others groundlessly without having considered what is possible, and therefore desiring to observe what we cannot. Next, it is possible that the moon's light derives from the moon

95   itself, or it comes from the sun. For on earth many things are seen by their own light, several by light from another source. And there is nothing in heavenly phenomena to contradict these explanations if we always keep in mind the method of multiple causes and make a comprehensive survey of hypotheses and causes consistent with the evidence, without looking to inconsistent explanations and granting them credibility without basis, or falling back, on various occasions and in different ways, on the method of the single cause.

"The Man in the Moon"

The impression of a face on the moon may be the result of a rearrangement of its parts or of something in between us and the moon, or of however many causes may be observed that are all consistent with the evidence of the

96   senses. In respect to all the heavenly bodies, we must not abandon this mode of investigation, for if we dispute the evident facts, we will never be able to partake of genuine peace of mind.

Solar and Lunar Eclipses

An eclipse of the sun and moon may occur as the result of their extinction, just as we see happen in our own experience, or again because of the interposition of certain other bodies, either Earth or an invisible body or something else of this kind. And in this way we ought to consider causes that are compatible with one another and realize that it is not impossible for more than a single cause to occur at the same time.

Their Regular Motions

Next, the regular motions of the heavenly bodies must be 97 understood as certain occurrences happen on earth. The divine should not be introduced in any way into these considerations, but kept free from duties and in all its blessedness. If this is not done, all speculation on the causes of heavenly phenomena will be in vain, as it has been already for certain parties who have not adhered to the method of possible explanation, but have slipped back into the useless way of thinking that things could happen in one way only. Rejecting all other possible causes, they are driven to unintelligible explanations and are unable to survey the phenomena that must be accepted as signs.

Night and Day

The alternating lengths of night and day may be due to 98 the movement of the sun, quick and then slow, above the earth, as it travels over areas of varying length or because it traverses some spots more quickly than others, just as can be observed in earthly phenomena, with which we must make valid comparisons when describing heavenly bodies. Those, on the other hand, who accept but a single cause do battle with the evidence and fail to ask whether it is possible for humankind to make observations.

THE WEATHER

Changes in the weather may be the result of the coincidence of occurrences, as is manifestly the case in the creatures around us, and changes and alterations in the at-
99   mosphere. Both these explanations are consonant with observable phenomena, but under what circumstances the change is owed to this or that cause, it is impossible to determine.

Clouds and Rain

Clouds may be produced and take shape as the result of the compression of air by the forcing together of winds and as the result of the interlacing of atoms that grip one another and are suitable to bringing about this result; and also because of the gathering of streams from earth and waters. And there are several other means by which the
100   formation of clouds can possibly occur. Now clouds' compression, on the one hand, and their undergoing a change, on the other, may produce rain, or else rain may result from a downward motion of winds moving through the air from appropriate quarters. A more violent shower may

result from a certain accumulation of atoms suited to create such a downpour.

Thunder and Lightning

Thunder may result both from the confinement of wind in the hollows of clouds, just as occurs in our own vessels, and the booming sound of fire filled with air inside of them, or else by the breakup of clouds that have congealed into a form like ice. Phenomena require us to admit that this event, like them all, occurs in various ways.

Just the same is lightning produced from many causes. 101 The atom that produces fire, escaping from the friction and collision of clouds, may give birth to lightning, or it may result from the winds' blowing forth from the clouds such atoms as make this flash; or else from a squeezing out of atoms when pressure in the clouds is produced either by each other or by winds. And again it may result from the gathering by the clouds of light dispersed from the stars. Or lightning occurs when the light that has the finest particles is strained through the clouds, whereby the clouds are burned by the fire and thunder results from the fire's motion. Or it occurs as a consequence of the firing of the 102 wind that results from the tension of its motion or its violent compression. Or the tearing of the clouds by wind may be responsible, and the expulsion of atoms that cause fire and produce the appearance of lightning. There are several other methods by which a man may arrive at these observations if he always keeps a firm hold on the evidence and can establish a theory in accordance with this.

Lightning precedes thunder in such a formation of

clouds because the lightning-producing atoms are thrust out at the same time as the wind bursts in and the wind later produces this roar; or because both lightning and thunder rush out of the cloud at the same time, but lightning travels toward us at a greater rate of speed, while thunder follows after, just as is the case of certain things seen from a distance and producing blows.*

It is possible that thunderbolts occur as the result of several gatherings of wind and a vehement whirling and a setting on fire with a portion of the fire breaking off and rushing violently toward places below. The breakup occurs because the regions through which the fire moves are successively denser due to the compression of clouds. Or thunderbolts may be the result of that same emission of fire by which thunder also can be produced, when the fire, growing too great and too violently filled with wind, tears the clouds apart because it cannot withdraw to the adjacent regions owing to the constant pressure of one cloud against another. Thunderbolts may be produced in several other ways. Only let mythical explanations not be admitted, and they will not be, if we make inferences about the unseen by attending closely to the visible.

Cyclones

Cyclones may be the result of the descent of a cloud in pillar form to the regions below by an incessant wind thrust inside it and carried along by this great wind, while at the same time wind from the outside drives the cloud sideways.

*I.e., if we see someone at a distance from us driving a hammer, we will see the blow of the hammer before we hear it.

Or they may result from a circular formation of wind, while a mist is being thrust down from above; or else from a great rush of wind that occurs and cannot pass through sideways because of the dense surrounding air. When the spout is let down over land, tornadoes develop in all the ways they may be created as a result of the wind's motion; over the sea, waterspouts result.   105

OTHER EARTHLY AND ATMOSPHERIC PHENOMENA

Earthquakes

Earthquakes may result both from the imprisonment of wind inside the earth, and from the earth's shifting in small masses and its constant movement, which produces the quaking. Either this wind enters in from outside; or, as a result of masses of earth falling into cave-like regions, the air trapped inside is fanned into wind. And again, earthquakes may be produced by the very distribution of the movement resulting from the fall of so many masses of earth and the returning shock whenever they encounter denser masses of earth. Earthquakes may also result from several other causes. . . .*   106

----

*Bailey marks a lacuna here, and argues that the following brief passage on winds "does not seem to be part of a general theory of wind . . . but rather of its origin in connexion with some other phenomenon." He suggests that the passage was once part of a section on volcanoes. See Bailey's note *ad loc.*

[Volcanoes]

Winds may result from time to time, when some foreign matter constantly and gradually slips in, and when an abundant amount of water collects. The remaining winds arise when a few fall into the many hollow places, and a distribution of wind occurs.

Hail

Hail results both from a rather violent congelation when certain windlike particles arise and then split up; and also from the more moderate congelation and simultaneous breakup of certain watery particles, which causes at the same time their compression and division, so that they 107 congeal both in separate parts and as a mass. It is not impossible that hail's curved or spherical shape results when the edges on all sides melt away and when in their conformation the particles, whether watery or windy, come together regularly, as the saying goes, part by part from all directions.

Snow

Snow may possibly result when a fine rain issues from the clouds through passages of convenient size and when there is a constant and strong compression of suitable clouds by the wind; then the water congeals in its descent due to a certain strong band of cold in the regions below the clouds. Or, due to a congealing in clouds that have a uniform porousness, an issuance of moisture of

this kind may result from the clouds of the watery kind
if they lie side by side and press against each other. Form-
ing a compression, as it were, they produce hail—something that often occurs in the atmosphere.* Or else, the   108
friction of clouds that have congealed may result in the
fall of an accumulation of snow. And there are several
other ways in which snow can be produced.

Dew, Frost, and Ice

Dew results both from the gathering of such elements as
are productive of such moisture from the atmosphere; and
from their being carried either from moist regions or regions that produce water, where dew most often is produced. The elements then meet, produce moisture, and are
carried back to the regions below, just as we see with phenomena in our experience. Frost results from a change   109
in these dew drops, some of them frozen in some way
owing to a surrounding of cold air.

Ice results both from the squeezing out of particles
with rounded configurations from the water, as the jagged
and sharp-angled elements that exist in the water come
together; and from the accretion of such outside particles
as make the water congeal when they are drawn together,
squeezing out a certain number of rounded particles.

---

*Usener reads *en toi eari* ("in the spring") for *en toi aeri* ("in
the atmosphere").

The Rainbow

The rainbow is caused by sunlight shining on watery air; or else as a result of a peculiar assimilation of light and air, which will produce the special properties of these colors, whether all together or separately. From the light, as it shines back, the adjacent portions of the air will assume the hue that we see, owing to the shining of the light on
10   its various parts. The rainbow's curved shape results from its entire surface being perceived at an equal distance from our eyes; or else it derives from the atoms in the air or those in the clouds that are reflected from the same air, assuming this shape as they combine and so present a kind of curve.

The Moon's Halo

A halo forms around the moon when air is carried from all sides toward the moon or when the air checks the current of light being carried away from the moon so evenly that it converts it into a circle of cloud and does not scatter it at all; or else the halo results when the air compresses the mist surrounding the moon evenly on all
111   sides and converts it into a rounded and dense shape. This occurs in certain parts of the sky either when a current of air presses hard from outside or when the heat stops up the passages in a way suitable to bringing about this effect.

MORE HEAVENLY PHENOMENA

Comets

Comets occur when fire is organized in certain places at certain times in the heavens when a gathering of matter takes place, or when at intervals the sky above us has a certain peculiar movement, resulting in the appearance of such stars. Or they themselves start to move at certain times due to some surrounding matter, and so they arrive at regions near to us and become visible. Their disappearance occurs for the opposite reasons.

Fixed Stars and Planets

Some stars "revolve in their place" (according to Homer),*   112
which happens not only because this part of the sky stands fixed while everything else revolves around it, as some men say, but also because a circular whirl of air surrounding it prevents these stars from moving about as the others do. Or else it may happen that there is not appropriate fuel for these stars everywhere, but only in that place where they are seen residing. And there are many other possible reasons for this, if one has the ability to make inferences that conform to the evidence.

    That some stars wander (if indeed they do happen   113
to move in such a way, while others do not move) may be due to the fact that moving in a circle from the beginning, they were so constrained that as a result some of

---

Iliad 18.487.

them are borne along the same uniform orbit but others in an orbit that has a certain irregularity. It is possible, on the other hand, that among the regions along which the stars are carried, there are uniform expanses of air propelling them constantly in the same direction and kindling them regularly, and elsewhere irregular spaces that result in the aberrations that we observe. But to assign a single cause to these occurrences, when the evidence we see demands a number of them, is madness and is properly practiced by those who are fanatically devoted to the idle notions of astrology, and who vainly assign causes to things, while they in no way absolve the divine nature of responsibility.

114   Some stars may be observed being left behind by others because they traverse the same orbit but are carried about more slowly, or because they move in the opposite direction, although drawn by the same revolution; or also because some stars are borne through a greater space and some through a smaller, although they follow the same circular path. But to offer a single account of these occurrences is the proper business of those who wish to perform marvels for the rabble.

Falling Stars

What are called falling stars may be produced partly by the stars' rubbing against each other and by the falling out of their fragments where a blast of wind occurs, just 115   as we said before about lightning; or else by a concurrence of fire-producing atoms, when their kindred material gathers to produce this, and by their movement in the direction of the impulse from the original concurrence. Falling stars may also result from a gathering of wind in certain mistlike concentrations, which is set on fire due to compression and which then bursts from its surroundings, as it is borne to that place toward which its motion impels it. And there are other explanations of these phenomena that are free from superstition.

WEATHER SIGNS

The signs certain animals give that indicate a change in the weather result from coincidence. For animals do not compel winter to come to an end, nor does some divine nature sit and observe when these animals venture out and then fulfill the signs they give. Such foolishness would not 116 befall a common creature, let alone a being possessed of perfect happiness.

CONCLUSION

Keep all these things in mind, Pythocles, for by so doing you will keep yourself free of superstition and be able to understand phenomena akin to these things I have told you about. Above all, devote yourself to the study of beginnings and infinitude and what is akin to them, and also of the criteria for judging and sensations, and the reasons why we reflect on these things. For these elements, when understood in their entirety, will enable you easily to comprehend the causes of particular details. But they who have not thoroughly assimilated these principles could not successfully comprehend them in themselves nor have they grasped why they should study these principles.

Letter to Menoeceus

INTRODUCTION

Let no one put off studying philosophy when he is young, ^{122*} nor when old grow weary of its study. For no one is too young or too far past his prime to achieve the health of his soul. The man who alleges that he is not yet ready for philosophy or that the time for it has passed him by, is like the man who says that he is either too young or too old for happiness. Therefore, we should study philosophy both in youth and in old age, so that we, though growing old, may be young in blessings through the pleasant memory of what has been; and when young we may be old as well, because we harbor no fear over what lies ahead. We must, therefore, pursue the things that make for happiness, seeing that when happiness is present, we have everything; but when it is absent, we do everything to possess it.

---

*In sections 117–121 of Book 10 of the *Lives,* Diogenes Laertius summarizes what Epicurus and his followers regard as the qualities inherent in the wise man, namely, kindness, sexual sobriety, loyalty to friends, and withdrawal from public life.

FIRST PRINCIPLES

The Gods

23   The things which I used constantly to recommend to you,
these things do and pursue, realizing that they are the
fundamental principles of the good life. First of all, regard
the god as an immortal and blessed being, as the concept
of deity is commonly presented, but do not apply to him
anything foreign to his immortality or out of keeping with
his blessedness; believe instead, concerning him, everything
that can safeguard his blessedness along with his immortality. For the gods exist; of them we have distinct knowledge.* But they are not such as the majority think them
to be. For they do not maintain a consistent view of what
they think the gods are. The impious man is not he who
confutes the gods of the majority, but he who applies to
24   the gods the majority's opinions. For the assertions of the
many concerning the gods are conceptions grounded not
in experience but in false assumptions, according to which
the greatest misfortunes are brought upon the evil by the
gods and the greatest benefits upon the good.† Men being

---

*Knowledge of the gods' existence proceeds from Epicurus' theory
of knowing: true knowledge derives from existing things; therefore,
a sure knowledge that the gods exist, which is shared by all men,
derives from the fact that gods *do* exist. Hence we can know about
them. For a discussion of the gods' nature, see, for example, Rist
1972: 145, and Jones 1989: 53–54.

†C. S. Lewis's description of Lucretius' atheism may serve as an
appropriate commentary here: "Lucretius was an atheist, and that is
precisely why he sees the beauty of the gods. . . . [I]t is *religio* [i.e.,
superstition] that hides them. . . . [T]he last taint of the sacrifice, and

always at home with their own virtues, they embrace those like themselves and regard everything unlike themselves as alien.

Death

Grow accustomed to the belief that death is nothing to us, since every good and evil lie in sensation. However, death is the deprivation of sensation. Therefore, correct understanding that death is nothing to us makes a mortal life enjoyable, not by adding an endless span of time but by taking away the longing for immortality. For there is nothing dreadful in life for the man who has truly comprehended that there is nothing terrible in not living. Therefore, foolish is the man who says that he fears death, not because it will cause pain when it arrives but because anticipation of it is painful. What is no trouble when it arrives is an idle worry in anticipation. Death, therefore— the most dreadful of evils—is nothing to us, since while we exist, death is not present, and whenever death is present, we do not exist. It is nothing either to the living or the dead, since it does not exist for the living, and the dead no longer are.

    The majority, however, sometimes flee from death as the greatest of evils, and other times choose it for themselves as a respite from the evils in life. The wise man neither rejects life nor fears not living. Life is not objectionable

125

126

of the urgent practical interest, the selfish prayer, must be washed away from them, before that other divinity can come to light in the imagination." C. S. Lewis, *The Allegory of Love: A Study of Medieval Tradition* (Oxford University Press, 1936): 83.

to him, nor is not living regarded as an evil. Just as he
assuredly chooses not the greatest quantity of food but
the most tasty, so does he enjoy the fruits not of the lengthiest
period of time but of the most pleasant.

He who advises the youth to live well but the old
man to die well is foolish, not only because of the desirability
of life but also because the training for living well and
dying well is the same. Much worse is he who says that
it is good not to be born and "once born to pass through
127   the gates of death as quickly as possible." If a man says
this with conviction, how can be avoid departing from life?
For this road is open to him, if he has firmly resolved
to do it. If, however, he has spoken in jest, he is considered
foolish among men who cannot welcome his words.

We must keep in mind that the future is neither completely ours nor not ours, so that we should not fully expect
it to come, nor lose hope, as if it were not coming at all.

THE MORAL THEORY

The Various Desires

We must consider that of the desires some are natural and
others idle: of the natural desires, some are necessary while
others are natural only. Of the necessary desires, there are
those that are necessary for happiness, those that are necessary for the body's freedom from disturbance, and those
128   that are necessary for life itself. A firm understanding of
these things enables us to refer every choice and avoidance
to the health of the body or the calm of the soul, since

this is the goal of a happy life. Everything we do is for the sake of this, namely, to avoid pain and fear. Once this is achieved, all the soul's trouble is dispelled, as the living being does not have to go in search of something missing or to seek something else, by which the good of the soul and of the body will be fulfilled. For we have need of pleasure at that time when we feel pain owing to the absence of pleasure. When we do not feel pain, it is because we no longer have need of pleasure. Therefore, we declare that pleasure is the beginning and the goal of a happy life. For we recognize pleasure as the first good 129 and as inborn; it is from this that we begin every choice and every avoidance. It is to pleasure that we have recourse, using the feeling as our standard for judging every good.

Pleasure and Pain

Since pleasure is the first good and natural to us, it is for this reason also that we do not choose every pleasure; instead, there are times when we pass over many pleasures, whenever greater difficulty follows from them. Also, we regard many pains as better than pleasures, since a greater pleasure will attend us after we have endured pain for a long time. Every pleasure, therefore, because of its natural relationship to us, is good, but not every pleasure is to be chosen. Likewise, every pain is an evil, but not every pain is of a nature always to be avoided. Yet it is proper 130 to judge all these things by a comparison and a consideration of both their advantages and disadvantages. For on certain occasions we treat the good as bad and, conversely, the bad as good.

Self-Sufficiency

We regard self-sufficiency as a great good, not that we may always have the enjoyment of but a few things, but that if we do not have many, we may have but few enjoyments in the genuine conviction that they take the sweetest pleasure in luxury who have least need of it, and that everything easy to procure is natural while everything difficult to obtain is superfluous. Plain dishes offer the same pleasure as a luxurious table, when the pain that comes from want is taken away. Bread and water offer the greatest pleasure when someone in need partakes of them. Becoming accustomed, therefore, to simple and not luxurious fare is productive of health and makes humankind resolved to perform the necessary business of life. When we approach luxuries after long intervals, it makes us better disposed toward them and renders us fearless of fortune.

131

Genuine Pleasure

When we say that pleasure is the goal, we are not talking about the pleasure of profligates or that which lies in sensuality, as some ignorant persons think, or else those who do not agree with us or have followed our argument badly; rather, it is freedom from bodily pain and mental anguish. For it is not continuous drinking and revels, nor the enjoyment of women and young boys, nor of fish and other viands that a luxurious table holds, which make for a pleasant life, but sober reasoning, which examines the motives for every choice and avoidance, and which drives away those opinions resulting in the greatest disturbance to the soul.

132

Prudence

The beginning and the greatest good of all these is prudence. For this reason prudence is more valuable even than philosophy: from it derive all the other virtues. Prudence teaches us how impossible it is to live pleasantly without living wisely, virtuously, and justly, just as we cannot live wisely, virtuously, and justly without living pleasantly. For the virtues arise naturally with the pleasant life; indeed, the pleasant life cannot be separated from them. Who, do   133 you think, is better than the man who keeps a reverent opinion about the gods, and is altogether fearless of death and has reasoned out the end of nature; who understands that the limit of good things is easy to attain and easy to procure, while the limit of evils is but brief in duration and small in pain; who laughs at fate, which is painted by some as the mistress over all things? . . .* Some things happen by necessity, others as the result of chance; other things are subject to our control. Because necessity is not accountable to anyone, he sees that chance is unstable, but what lies in our control is subject to no master; it naturally follows, then, that blame or praise attend our decisions.

Indeed, it would be better to accept the myths about   134 the gods than to be a slave to the "destiny" of the physical philosophers. The myths present the hope of appeasing the gods through worship, while the other is full of unappeasable necessity. Understanding that chance is neither a god, as the majority think (for nothing is done

---

*There is a gap in the text here, and what follows immediately is uncertain.

by a god in an irregular fashion), nor an unstable cause of all things, the wise man does not think that either good or evil is furnished by chance to humankind for the purpose of living a happy life, but that the opportunities for great
35 good or evil are bestowed by it. He thinks that it is preferable to remain prudent and suffer ill fortune than to enjoy good luck while acting foolishly. It is better in human actions that the sound decision fail than that the rash decision turn out well due to luck.

CONCLUSION

Take thought, then, for these and kindred matters day and night, on your own or in the company of someone like yourself. You shall be disturbed neither waking nor sleeping, and you shall live as a god among men. For the man who dwells among immortal blessings is not like a mortal being.

Principal Doctrines

1. The blessed and immortal is itself free from trouble nor   139*
does it cause trouble for anyone else; therefore, it is not
constrained either by anger or by favor. For such sentiments
exist only in the weak.

2.† Death is nothing to us. For what has been dispersed
has no sensation. And what has no sensation is nothing
to us.

3. The limit of the extent of pleasure is the removal of
all pain. Wherever pleasure is present, for however long
a time, there can be no pain or grief, or both at once.

4. Pain does not dwell continuously in the flesh. Extreme   140
pain is present but a very brief time, and that which barely
exceeds bodily pleasure continues no more than a few days.
But chronic illness allows greater pleasure than pain in
the flesh.

---

*These follow a brief passage in Diogenes Laertius' *Lives* (10.135–
138), in which he describes how Epicurus' teachings about pleasure differ
from those of the Cyrenaics, and then introduces the *Principal Doctrines*.
    †Cf. the letter to Menoeceus, sec. 124.

5.* It is impossible to live pleasantly without living prudently, well, and justly, nor is it possible to live prudently, well, and justly without living pleasantly. The man for whom this latter condition is impossible cannot live prudently, well, or justly; he for whom the former is impossible, cannot live pleasantly.

6. Whatever you can provide yourself with to secure protection from men is a natural good.

141 7. Some men wished to become esteemed and admired by everyone, thinking that in this way they would procure for themselves safety from others. Therefore, if the life of such men is safe, they have received the good that comes from nature. If it is not safe, they do not have that for which they struggled at first by natural instinct.

8. No pleasure is evil in itself; but the means of obtaining some pleasures bring in their wake troubles many times greater than the pleasures.

142 9. If every pleasure were condensed† and existed for a long time throughout the entire organism or its most important parts, pleasures would never differ from one another.

10. If the things that beget pleasure in dissolute individuals could dispel their minds' fears about the heavens, death, and pain, and could still teach them the limits of desires, we would have no grounds for finding fault with the dissolute, since they would be filling themselves with

---

*Cf. the letter to Menoeceus, sec. 132.

†By "condensed" here, Epicurus means "maximized."

pleasures from every source and in no way suffering from pain or grief, which are evil.

11. If apprehensions about the heavens and our fear lest death concern us, as well as our failure to realize the limits of pains and desires, did not bother us, we would have no need of natural science.

12. It is impossible for anyone to dispel his fear over the most important matters, if he does not know what is the nature of the universe but instead suspects something that happens in myth. Therefore, it is impossible to obtain un-mitigated pleasure without natural science.   143

13. There is no benefit in securing protection from men if things above and beneath the earth and indeed all the limitless universe are made matters for suspicion.

14. The most perfect means of securing safety from men, which arises, to some extent, from a certain power to expel, is the assurance that comes from quietude and withdrawal from the world.

15. Natural wealth is limited and easily obtained; the riches of idle fancies go on forever.   144

16. In few instances does chance intrude upon the wise man, but reason has administered his greatest and most important affairs, and will continue to do so throughout his whole life.

17. The just man is most free of perturbation, while the unjust man is full of the greatest disturbance.

18. The pleasure in the flesh will not be increased when once the pain resulting from want is taken away, but only varied. The limit of understanding as regards pleasure is obtained by a reflection on these same pleasures and the sensations akin to them, which used to furnish the mind with its greatest fears.

145   19. Infinite time contains the same amount of pleasure as finite time, if one measures the limits of pleasure by reason.

20. The flesh considers the limits of pleasure to be boundless, and only infinite time makes it possible. But the mind, having gained a reasonable understanding of the end and limit of the flesh, and having expelled fears about eternity, furnishes the complete life, and we no longer have any need for time without end. But the mind does not flee from pleasure nor, when circumstances bring about the departure from life, does it take its leave as though falling short somehow of the best life.

146   21. He who understands the limits of life knows how easy it is to remove the pain that results from want and to make one's whole life complete. As a result, he does not need actions that bring strife in their wake.

22. We must take into account both the underlying purpose and all the evidence of clear perception, to which we refer our opinions. Otherwise, everything will be filled with confusion and indecision.

23. If you do battle with all your sensations, you will be unable to form a standard for judging even which of them you judge to be false.

24. If you reject any sensation and you do not distinguish   147
between the opinion based on what awaits confirmation
and evidence already available based on the senses, the
feelings, and every intuitive faculty of the mind, you will
send the remaining sensations into a turmoil with your
foolish opinions, thus driving out every standard for judging.
And if, among the perceptions based on opinion, you affirm
both that which awaits confirmation and that which does
not, you will fail to escape from error, since you will have
retained every ground for dispute in judgment concerning
right and wrong.

25. If you do not on every occasion refer each of your   148
actions to the end ordained by nature, but instead stop
short at something else when considering whether to go
after something or avoid it, your actions will not be in
keeping with the principles you profess.

26. Those desires that do not lead to pain, if they are not
fulfilled, are not necessary. They involve a longing that
is easily dispelled, whenever it is difficult to fulfill the desires
or they appear likely to lead to harm.

27. Of all the things that wisdom provides for living one's
entire life in happiness, the greatest by far is the possession
of friendship.

28. The same knowledge that makes one confident that
nothing dreadful is eternal or long-lasting, also recognizes
in the face of these limited evils the security afforded by
friendship.

29. Of the desires some are natural and necessary while   149
others are natural but unnecessary. And there are desires

that are neither natural nor necessary but arise from idle opinion.

30. If there is intense striving after those physical desires that do not lead to pain if unfulfilled, this is because they arise from idle opinion; they fail to be dispelled, not because of their own nature but because of the vain fancies of humankind.

|50 31. Natural justice is a pledge guaranteeing mutual advantage, to prevent one from harming others and to keep oneself from being harmed.

32. For those living creatures that are unable to form compacts not to harm others or to be harmed, there is neither justice nor injustice. It is the same for all tribes of men unable or unwilling to form compacts not to do harm or be harmed.

33. There is no such thing as "justice in itself"; it is, rather, always a certain compact made during men's dealings with one another in different places, not to do harm or to be harmed.

151 34. Injustice is not evil in itself but in the fear and apprehension that one will not escape from those appointed to punish such actions.

35. It is impossible for the one who commits some act in secret violation of the compacts made among men not to do harm or to be harmed, to remain confident that he will escape notice, even if for the present he escapes detection a thousand times. For right up to the day of his death, it remains unclear whether he will escape detection.

36. Broadly considered, justice is the same for all, because it is a kind of mutual benefit in men's interactions with one another. But in individual countries and circumstances, justice turns out not to be the same for all.

37. Among the measures regarded as just, that which is proven to be beneficial in the business of men's dealings with one another, has the guarantee of justice whether it is the same for all or not. If someone makes a law which does not result in advantage for men's dealings with each other, it no longer has the nature of justice. Even if advantage in the matter of justice is variable but nonetheless conforms for a certain length of time to the common notion people have of it, no less for that period is it just in the opinion of those who do not confuse themselves with words but look straight at the facts. 152

38. Where actions that were considered just are shown not to fit the conception (of justice) in actual practice—provided circumstances are not altered—they are not just. But where, once events have changed, the same actions once held to be just are no longer advantageous, they were just at the time when they brought advantage to citizens' dealings with one another; but later they were no longer just, when they brought no advantage. 153

39. The man who has best settled the feeling of disquiet that comes from external circumstances is he who has made those things he can of the same kin as himself; and what he cannot, at least not alien. Whatever he cannot do even this to he avoids all contact with, and banishes whatever it is advantageous to treat in this way. 154

40. Those who possess the power of securing themselves completely from their neighbors, live most happily with one another, since they have this constant assurance. And after partaking of the fullest intimacy, they do not mourn a friend who dies before they do, as though there were need for pity.

Vatican Sayings

4.* All physical pain is negligible: that which is intense lasts but a brief time, while chronic physical discomfort has no great intensity.†

7.‡ It is difficult for a wrongdoer to go undetected; to remain assured that he will go undetected is impossible.

9.** Necessity is an evil thing, but there is no necessity to live beneath the yoke of necessity.

10. Remember that you are mortal and that, although having but a limited span of life, you have entered into discussions about nature for an eternity and forever, and seen "all things that are and will be and were before."††

11. The leisure time of most men numbs them; activity drives them mad.

---

*Nos. 1–3 = *Principal Doctrines* 1, 2, and 4.
†Cf. *Principal Doctrines* 4, of which this is a summary.
‡Nos. 5 and 6 = *Principal Doctrines* 5 and 35.
**No. 8 = *Principal Doctrines* 15.
††Homer, *Iliad* 1. 70.

14.* We are born once and cannot be born twice, but we must be no more for all time. Not being master of tomorrow, you nonetheless delay your happiness. Life is consumed by procrastination, and each of us dies without providing leisure for himself.

15. We honor our characters as if they were distinctive to ourselves, whether we have worthy characters and are admired by men or not. Therefore, we must esteem the characters of our neighbors, if they are friendly toward us.

16. No one, when he sees evil, chooses it for himself, but enticed by it as though a good in comparison with a greater evil, he hunts after it.

17. Not the youth, but the old man who has lived life well, is to be deemed happy. The youth in his prime is made distraught and baffled by fortune; the old man, as though in port in his old age, has brought safely into harbor the goods he scarcely hoped for before, and has secured them with unfailing gratitude.

18. When sight is taken away along with association and intercourse, erotic passion ceases.

19. Not remembering the past good, he has become an old man this day.

21.† We must not resist nature but obey her. We shall obey her by fulfilling the necessary desires and the physical ones if they do not harm us, but harshly rejecting the harmful ones.

---

*Nos. 12 and 13 = *Principal Doctrines* 17 and 27.
†No. 20 = *Principal Doctrines* 19.

23.* All friendship is desirable for itself, but it begins with need.

24. Dreams possess neither a divine nature nor prophetic power. They arise from the impact of images.

25. When measured by the natural purpose of life, poverty is great wealth; limitless wealth, great poverty.

26. One must perceive that both the long speech and the short one tend toward the same end.

27. In other occupations, the reward comes with difficulty after their completion, but in philosophy delight coincides with knowledge. For enjoyment does not come after learning, but learning and enjoyment come together.

28. We should approve neither those always eager for friendship, nor those who hang back. It is necessary even to run risks for friendship's sake.

29. Speaking frankly, I would prefer, when discoursing on nature, to utter useful things, like oracles, to humankind, even if no one should understand them, than to agree with popular opinion and enjoy the constant accolades offered by the crowd.

30. Some men spend their whole life furnishing for themselves the things proper to life without realizing that at our birth each of us was poured a mortal brew to drink.

31. Against all else it is possible to provide security; but as far as death is concerned, we all dwell in an unfortified city.

---

*No. 22 = *Principal Doctrines* 19.

32. Among those who revere him, the veneration of the wise man is a great good.

33. The voice of the flesh cries, "Keep me from hunger, thirst, and cold!" The man who has these sureties and who expects he always will would rival even Zeus for happiness.

34. We do not need the help of our friends so much as the confidence that our friends will help us.

35. We must not spoil our present estate by longing for what is absent but realize that this, too, was one of the things we hoped for.

36. The life of Epicurus, when compared with those of others, might be considered legendary for its gentleness and self-sufficiency.*

37. Nature is weak when it comes to evil, but not when it comes to good; for it is saved by pleasure but destroyed by pains.

38. He is a little man in every way, for whom there are many persuasive reasons for departing from life.

39. The man continually seeking help is no friend, nor is the one who never links help with friendship. For the one barters kindness for favors, while the other cuts off hope for the future.

40. The man who says that everything happens by necessity cannot quarrel with another who denies that every-

---

*Bailey's note *ad loc.*: "This fragment clearly cannot be attributed to Epicurus himself. Usener would assign it to Hermarchus, his successor as head of the school."

thing happens by necessity, for he affirms that this, too, happens by necessity.

41. At the same time, we must laugh, philosophize, manage our households, take care of our other private affairs, and never cease proclaiming the sayings born of true philosophy.

42. The time of the beginning and enjoyment of the greatest good is the same.

43. To love ill-gotten wealth is impious; to love wealth justly earned is shameful. For even with justice on your side, it is unseemly to be thrifty to the point of meanness.

44. The wise man who has accustomed himself to the bare necessities knows how to give rather than to receive. So great is the treasure house of self-sufficiency he has discovered.

45. The study of nature does not make men practice boastful speech or display a learning highly coveted by the rabble; rather, it makes men modest and self-sufficient, taking pride in the good that lies in themselves, not in their estate.

46. Let us completely drive away foul habits, as we would base men who have done us great harm for a long time.

47. I have anticipated you, Fortune, and have barred your means of entry. Neither to you nor to any other circumstance shall we hand ourselves over as captives. But when necessity compels us, we shall depart from life, spitting on it and on those who vainly cling to it, declaring in a beautiful song of triumph how well we have lived.

48. As long as we are on the road (of life), we must make the later journey better than the beginning, but be happy and content when we have reached the end.

51.* I hear from you that carnal appetites make you too eager for sexual pleasures. If you do not break the laws, disturb well-established customs, upset any of your neighbors, do bodily harm to yourself, or waste your resources, give in to your inclinations as you please. However, you cannot avoid being impeded by one of these barriers. For sexual pleasure has never done anybody any good. One must be content if it has not done actual harm.

52. Friendship dances around the world proclaiming to us all to rouse ourselves to give thanks.

53. We must envy no one. Good men do not deserve envy; as for the wicked, the more good luck they have, the more they inflict pain on themselves.

54. We must not pretend to be philosophers, but be philosophers in truth. For we do not stand in need of the appearance of health but of true health.

55. We must tend to our misfortunes by the happy memory of what is gone and by the realization that it is impossible to undo what has been done.

56. The wise man suffers no more pain by being tortured himself than by seeing a friend being tortured.

57. (The wise man's) whole life will be confounded and upset by deceit.

---

*Nos. 49 and 50 = *Principal Doctrines* 12 and 8.

58. We must free ourselves from the prison of everyday affairs and politics.

59. The stomach is not insatiable, as many people say, but rather the false opinion that the stomach needs an endless amount to fill it.

60. Everyone departs from life as if he had only just been born.

61. Most beautiful is the sight of those near to us when primary kinship is of one mind—a thing that is very eager to secure this end.

62. If parents are rightfully angry with their children, it is, of course, useless for the children to resist and not beg their forgiveness; but if parents have no just or logical reason for their anger, it is foolish for the child to inflame their unreason further by nursing his own anger and not to seek, by being considerate, to turn aside their wrath through other means.

63. There is also a limit to frugality. The man unable to consider this suffers a similar end as the man who indulges in excess.

64. Praise from others must follow of its own accord; our object should be our own healing.

65. It is useless to ask the gods for what one is capable of obtaining for oneself.

66. Let us show feeling for our friends not by lamenting but by reflection.*

---

*I.e., reflecting on the lives of friends who have died.

67. A life of freedom cannot acquire many possessions, since to accomplish this requires servility to the rabble or to kings; but such a life possesses everything in unfailing supply. If somehow such a life does happen to acquire many possessions, it will also know how to distribute these to win the neighbors' good will.

68. Nothing is sufficient for the man to whom the sufficient is too little.

69. The thankless greed of the soul makes the creature forever hungry for refinements in its mode of living.

70. You ought to do nothing in your life that will make you afraid if it becomes known to your neighbor.

71. The following method of inquiry must be applied to every desire: What will happen to me if what I long for is accomplished? What will happen if it is not accomplished?

73.* Our experience of certain bodily pains helps us to guard against a similar occurrence of them.

74. The one who is beaten in a philosophical discussion gains more the more he learns.

75. Ungrateful for past benefits is the saying, "Look to the end of a long life."

76. You are, as you grow old, the man I urge you to be, and you have distinguished between pursuing knowl-

---

*No. 72 = *Principal Doctrines* 13.

edge for your own sake and pursuing it for Greece. I congratulate you.*

77. The greatest fruit of self-sufficiency is freedom.

78. The noble man is most concerned with wisdom and friendship. Of these one is a mortal good, the other immortal.

79. The tranquil man is not troublesome to himself or to another.

80. The first measure of salvation is to keep watch over one's youth and to guard against those forces that sully everything with the rage of passion.

81. The possession of the greatest riches does not resolve the agitation of the soul or give birth to remarkable joy —nor does the honor and admiration of the crowd, nor any other of those things arising from unlimited desires.

---

*This may be a fragment of a letter by Epicurus to an older disciple, possibly Leonteus of Lampsacus (see Bailey's note *ad loc.*).

Fragments

FRAGMENTS FROM IDENTIFIABLE WORKS

I. On Choice and Avoidance

1. Peace of mind and freedom from bodily pain are static pleasures; joy and gladness, however, are regarded as active emotions, in accordance with their motility.

II. Problems

2. Will the wise man do things forbidden by law, knowing that he will not be caught? The simple answer is not easy to find.

III. The Brief Epitome*

3. There is no such thing as prophecy and, even if there were, what comes to pass ought to be regarded by us as nothing.

---

*The letter to Herodotus, also known as the Lesser Epitome, contains no reference to prophecy. Bailey conjectures that such a refer-

IV. Against Theophrastus

4. But even apart from this matter, I do not know how we ought to say that objects that are in darkness possess color.*

V. Symposium

5. *Polyaenus.*† Are you denying, Epicurus, the warming effect of wine? (Someone took up the discourse): Wine does not appear unnconditionally to produce warmth. (And a little later): It appears that wine does not appear unconditionally to produce warmth; however, a sufficient quantity of wine might be said to produce a feeling of warmth in a certain person.
6. Therefore, we must not say that wine produces warmth unconditionally, but that a certain quantity of wine produces warmth in one constitution that is so disposed to it, while in another it produces a feeling of cold. For there are in the composite body of wine such properties from which cold may be produced if, as needs be, they are joined with

---

ence dropped out or that this fragment, which also occurs in Diogenes Laertius' *Life of Epicurus,* sec. 134, has been mistakenly ascribed to the Lesser Epitome.

*This has to do with Epicurus' argument about properties and accidents that are attached to bodies (cf. the letter to Herodotus, sec. 68 ff.). It has been debated whether color is an essential property. As Rist 1972: 65, argues: "To point out that if we look at [an object] in the dark, the colours have disappeared, is unhelpful. We should only have to worry about whether colour was a primary quality if when we put the object back in the light, it still appeared uncoloured."

†Polyaenus was a famed mathematician and member of Epicurus' school.

other properties to produce a feeling of cold. Therefore, those claiming that wine is unconditionally productive of cold or heat are mistaken.

7. Often wine enters the body without bringing with it the power to heat or to cool; but if the body's mass is disturbed and there occurs a rearrangement of atoms, those atoms that produce a feeling of warmth now gather into one place and provide a sense of warmth and inflammation to the body, owing to their number. And now as they withdraw, they leave a feeling of cold.

8. Sexual intercourse has never conferred a benefit; one should reckon oneself glad if it has not brought any harm.*

9. It is a wonder indeed, if you were not impeded because of your youth—as you yourself would admit—from rising above everyone (young as you are), even your distinguished elders, in the art of speaking . . . a marvel indeed, if you have not been impeded because of your youth from distinguishing yourself in skill at speaking,† which seems to be a matter of care and a great deal of practice. But it is possible to be impeded, owing to one's youth, from seeing reality as it is, for which knowledge would appear to be responsible rather than practice and care.

VI. Concerning the Ends of Life

10. For my part I do not know how I shall conceive the good, if I take away the pleasures of taste, if I take away

---

*Cf. *Vatican Sayings* 51.

†I have altered the language somewhat, but in the Greek the words are virtually the same, possibly indicating some unnecessary duplication or a conflation of two similar passages.

sexual pleasure, if I take away the pleasure of hearing, and if I take away the sweet emotions that are caused by the sight of a beautiful form.

11. A stable physical condition and assurance of its continuance furnish the highest and most certain joy for those who are able to take it into account.

12. Let beauty and pleasure and suchlike be honored if they provide pleasure; if they do not provide pleasure, let them go.

VII. On Nature

Book 1

13. The nature of the universe is bodies and void.
14. The nature of existing things is bodies and space.

Book 11

15. If (the sun) had been reduced in size because of the space (between it and us), much more would it have lost its color; for no other distance is better suited to this reduction.*

---

*See Bailey's note *ad loc.*: "This fragment . . . must be compared with Lucr[etius] v. 564 ff., where it is argued that terrestrial lights become confused in outline before they appear to diminish in size. Much more so would this happen with the sun whose great distance from the earth would be very likely to cause such blurring. But the outline of the sun is not blurred. Therefore we must suppose that his size is not diminished."

FRAGMENTS FROM UNCERTAIN WORKS

16. An atom is a solid body having no admixture of void. Void is an impalpable existence.*

17. But let them go. For he, as though in the travail of childbirth, kept issuing from his mouth sophistical boasting, like many other slaves.†

FRAGMENTS OF LETTERS

18. If they have this in mind, they are prevailing over the evils that attend want and poverty.

19. Even if there is a war,‡ he will not reckon it a dreadful thing if the gods are merciful. He has led and, if the gods are merciful, will lead an unblemished life in company with Matro.

20. Tell me, Polyaenus, do you know what has been a great joy to us?

---

*Atoms and void are discussed at greater length in the letter to Herodotus, sec. 40. The void cannot be "felt" as bodies can, but its existence can be inferred. In his work *On the Nature of the Gods* 1.54, Cicero indicates that atoms and void are understood by contact of the mind (see Rist 1972: 36).

†This passage recurs in Diogenes Laertius' *Life of Epicurus*, sec. 7, where there is a reference to Nausiphanes of Teos. Epicurus, however, treats him with scorn.

‡I am not sure what the "war" here refers to, although it may allude generally to the suppression of the independent Greek city-states by Macedon following the death of Alexander; or it may refer more specifically to the quarrels between Epicurus and his rival philosophers.

Letters Addressed to Several Persons

To the Philosophers in Mytilene

21. These things drove him to such distraction that he railed at me and disparagingly called me a teacher.*
22. I suppose that these abusive persons will think that I am a pupil of the jellyfish,† and that I attend him in the company of certain debauched youths. For indeed he was a scoundrel and practitioner of such things that cannot lead to wisdom.

Letters to Individuals

To Anaxarchus

23. I shall summon you to constant pleasures and not to empty and foolish distinctions with their unsettling expectations of rewards.

To Apelles

24. I congratulate you, Apelles, for having pursued philosophy free of all taint.

---

*Another reference to Nausiphanes (cf. Diogenes Laertius, *Lives of the Eminent Philosophers* 10.8).
†Still another abusive reference to Nausiphanes.

*To Themista**

25. If you two do not come to me, I am capable of being persuaded to rush on my own to wherever you and Themista summon me.

To Idomeneus†

26. Send us offerings on behalf of yourself and your children for the nurture of our sacred body. Thus does it occur to me to speak.
27. O you who have regarded, from your youth, all my urgings as delightful . . .
28. If you want to make Pythocles a rich man, do not add to his store but take away his desire.
29. We esteem self-sufficiency not so that we may always prefer the cheap and the frugal, but so that we may feel no dread regarding them.
30. As I spend this happy day at the end of my life, I write this to you. Strangury and dysentery are dogging me with all their usual intensity. But this pain yields to the joy in my heart at the recollection of the conversations I have had with you. You in turn, in a manner worthy of your affection for me since childhood as well as of your devotion to philosophy, take good care of the children of Metrodorus.‡

---

*The wife of Leonteus, both disciples of Epicurus.
†One of Epicurus' leading disciples.
‡The Metrodorus mentioned here is a devoted friend and pupil of Epicurus; he is already dead and the master wishes to celebrate his memory. See Bailey's note *ad loc.*

To Colotes*

31. As though in reverence for the things I have said, you have been overtaken by an inexplicable longing to grasp and embrace my knees and to manifest the usual signs that attend the reverence and prayers due certain persons. Therefore, you have made me consecrate and revere you in turn. Go live now as a god and regard us, too, as immortal.

To Leontion†

32. Lord and savior, my dear Leontion, what a desire for applause you filled me with as I read your sweet letter.

To Pythocles

33. Blessed youth, board your skiff and flee from all education.‡

34. I shall sit and await your lovely and godlike appearance.

---

*A student of Epicurus who wrote an attack on rival schools of philosophy. The tone of this fragment is ironic, but it is apparent that Epicurus achieved the status of a "holy man" among his followers; cf. no. 26, the fragment to Idomeneus, and see also Lucretius 3.7–14 for an example of the consecration of Epicurus' memory.

†Reputedly the wife or concubine of Metrodorus; see fragment 30, above.

‡What is meant here is a typical Athenian education. Epicurus claimed independence from all other philosophical schools.

Letters to Uncertain Persons

To a Boy or Girl

35. We have arrived safely at Lampsacus, Pythocles, Hermarchus, Ctesippus, and I, and there we found Themista and our other friends in good health. I trust you, too, and your mama are well and in good health, and that you obey your papa and Matro in all things, just as you used to. You're well aware of why I and all the others love you so—because you obey them in all things.

Letter Written at the End of Epicurus' Life

36. A week before I wrote this, I could not pass my urine and there was pain such as bring men to their final day. If anything happens to me, take charge of the children of Metrodorus for four or five years, but at no greater expense than you allot to me for one year.

Fragments of Various Letters

37. I revel with pleasure in the body, living as I do on bread and water; I spit on extravagant pleasures, not for themselves but for the difficulties that attend them.
38. As I told you when you were departing, take care, too, of his brother Apollodorus. While he is not a bad boy, he gives me concern when he does something he does not mean to do.
39. Send me a pot of cheese, so that I may be able to indulge myself whenever I wish.

40. You have taken marvelous and splendid care of me by supplying me with food, and you have shown signs that reach to heaven of your kindness toward me.

41. The pension which . . . ordered sent to me even in the land of the Hyperboreans,* this and this alone I require; from each of you, I wish to receive only 120 drachmas a year. . . .

Ctesippus has brought the annual pension which you sent on behalf of your father and yourself.

42. He will have as a valuable return the education I have given him.

43. I never desired to please the rabble. What pleased them, I did not learn; and what I knew was far removed from their understanding.

44. Do not think it unusual that when the flesh cries out, the soul cries as well. The cry of the flesh is not to hunger or thirst, not to be cold.† It is difficult for the soul to hinder these cries, and dangerous for it to disregard the summons of nature because of the soul's natural independence day by day.

45. He who follows nature and not idle opinions is independent in all things. As far as concerns what suffices for nature, every acquisition is wealth; but when it comes to unlimited desires, even the greatest wealth (is not wealth but poverty).

46. Your anxiety is in direct proportion to your forgetfulness of nature, for you bring on yourself unlimited fears and desires.

48.‡ (spoken to a woman) It is better for you to be free

---

*A people who supposedly lived in the far north.
†Cf. *Vatican Sayings* 33.
‡No. 47 = *Vatican Sayings* 14.

of fear and lying on a bed of straw than to own a couch of gold and a lavish table and yet have no peace of mind.

49. . . . bearing the letter from you and your discussion about the men who can see neither the analogy between phenomena and the invisible nor the harmony that exists between sensations and the invisible and again the counter-evidence. . . .

50. Sweet is the memory of a dead friend.

51. Do not avoid granting small favors, for it will make you seem the sort of person to confer great ones.

52. If an enemy asks a favor, do not scorn his request. Only keep on your guard, for he is no different from a dog.

FRAGMENTS WHOSE SOURCE IS UNCERTAIN

On Philosophy

54.* Vain is the word of a philosopher, by which no mortal suffering is healed. Just as medicine confers no benefit if it does not drive away bodily disease, so is philosophy useless if it does not drive away the suffering of the mind.

Physics

55. Nothing new can happen in the universe, as compared to the infinite span of time that has already passed.

56. We shall not regard them as more blessed and inde-

---

*No. 53 = *Vatican Sayings* 54.

structible if they neither speak nor converse with one another, but rather as deaf and dumb men.

57. Let us at least offer pious and noble sacrifice where it is customary, and let us do everything well according to the law without upsetting ourselves over beliefs in what constitutes ᵗʰe highest and most sacred. Furthermore, let us be righteous without need of inspiration by beliefs that others proclaim, for thus is it possible to live in accordance with nature.

58. If the gods listened to the prayers of men, all humankind would quickly perish since they constantly pray for many evils to befall one another.

Ethics

59. The beginning and root of every good is the pleasure of the stomach. Even wisdom and refinements are referable to this.

60. We have need of pleasure when we suffer pain because of pleasure's absence. But when we are not suffering this pain, although in a state of sensation, there is no need for pleasure. For it is not natural pleasure that sets wrongdoing into action, but rather the striving after idle fancies.

61. That which creates unsurpassable joy is the removal of a great evil. And this is the nature of good if one grasps it correctly and then holds steadily to it, without walking about* uttering vain rubbish about the good.

62. It is better to endure these particular pains so that we may feel greater pleasures. It is good to refrain from

---

*The Greek here is *peripatē,* which may be a veiled reference to Aristotle's Peripatetic School of philosophy.

these particular pleasures so that we may not suffer more difficult pains.

63. Let us not blame the flesh as the cause of great evils nor refer our misfortunes to circumstances.

64. Great pains quickly carry us off; chronic pains, however, are not severe.

65. Excessive pain will border on death.

66. By love of true philosophy are we delivered from every disturbing and painful desire.

67. Thanks be to blessed nature for making the necessary easy to secure and the unnecessary difficult to supply.

68. It is not unusual to find a man (poor) in determining the true purpose of life but rich in vain fancies. No fool is satisfied with what he has, but instead grieves for what he does not possess. Just as men with fevers are always thirsty because of the malignant character of their illness, and desiring the opposite of what is good for them, so are those of an evil frame of mind always poor in everything and are impelled by their greed toward various desires.

69. He who is not satisfied with a little, is satisfied with nothing.*

70. Self-sufficiency is the greatest of all wealth.

71. Many a man, fearing a mean style of living, is driven, because of his fear, to adopt practices that are most conducive to fear.

72. Many men who acquire wealth do not find deliverance from evils but an exchange of their present evils for greater ones.

---

*Cf. *Vatican Sayings* 68.

73. Great abundance is heaped up as the result of brutalizing labor, but a miserable life is the result.

74. A person is made unhappy either by fear or by endless and vain desire. The man who curbs these can attain for himself the blessed gift of reason.

75. Being deprived of these things is no hardship; rather, it is the endurance of useless pain that results from idle fancies.

76. The mean soul is puffed up by successes, but brought down by adversity.

77. (Nature) teaches us to regard what fortune brings as of little worth; to recognize, when we are well off, that we are unfortunate; when we are not prosperous, to regard prosperity as of little worth; and to receive without excess emotion the goods that fortune bestows and to stand prepared to face its seeming evils. Know that what passes for good and evil among the throng is ephemeral, and that wisdom shares nothing in common with fortune.

78. He who has least need of tomorrow will most gladly greet tomorrow.

79. I spit on the beautiful and those who idly gawk at it, if it produces no pleasure.

80. Justice's greatest reward is peace of mind.

81. The laws are laid down for the sake of the wise, not to prevent them from doing wrong but to keep them from being wronged.

82. Even if they are able to escape detection, it is impossible for them to remain assured of escaping. Therefore, fear over the future always presses upon them and does not allow them to take pleasure or confidence in the present.

83. The man who has realized the highest purpose of

the human race is equally as good, even when no one is around.

84. It is impossible for the one who instills fear to remain free from fear.

85. Happiness and blessedness do not belong to abundance of riches or exalted position or offices or power, but to freedom from pain and gentleness of feeling and a state of mind that sets limits that are in accordance with nature.

86. Live your life without attracting attention.

87. We must say how a person will best observe the purpose of life, and how one will not willingly at first pursue public office.

GREAT MINDS PAPERBACK SERIES

ART

❏ Leonardo da Vinci—*A Treatise on Painting*

ECONOMICS

❏ Charlotte Perkins Gilman—*Women and Economics: A Study of the Economic Relation between Women and Men*
❏ John Maynard Keynes—*The End of Laissez-Faire* and *The Economic Consequences of the Peace*
❏ John Maynard Keynes—*The General Theory of Employment, Interest, and Money*
❏ John Maynard Keynes—*A Tract on Monetary Reform*
❏ Thomas R. Malthus—*An Essay on the Principle of Population*
❏ Alfred Marshall—*Money, Credit, and Commerce*
❏ Alfred Marshall—*Principles of Economics*
❏ Karl Marx—*Theories of Surplus Value*
❏ John Stuart Mill—*Principles of Political Economy*
❏ David Ricardo—*Principles of Political Economy and Taxation*
❏ Adam Smith—*Wealth of Nations*
❏ Thorstein Veblen—*The Theory of the Leisure Class*

HISTORY

❏ Edward Gibbon—*On Christianity*
❏ Alexander Hamilton, John Jay, and James Madison—*The Federalist*
❏ Herodotus—*The History*
❏ Charles Mackay—*Extraordinary Popular Delusions and the Madness of Crowds*
❏ Thucydides—*History of the Peloponnesian War*

LAW

❏ John Austin—*The Province of Jurisprudence Determined*

LITERATURE

❏ Jonathan Swift—*A Modest Proposal and Other Satires*
❏ H. G. Wells—*The Conquest of Time*

POLITICS

❏ Walter Lippmann—*A Preface to Politics*

PSYCHOLOGY

❏ Sigmund Freud—*Totem and Taboo*

RELIGION/FREETHOUGHT

❏ Desiderius Erasmus—*The Praise of Folly*
❏ Thomas Henry Huxley—*Agnosticism and Christianity and Other Essays*
❏ Ernest Renan—*The Life of Jesus*
❏ Upton Sinclair—*The Profits of Religion*
❏ Elizabeth Cady Stanton—*The Woman's Bible*

❑ Voltaire—*A Treatise on Toleration and Other Essays*
❑ Andrew D. White—*A History of the Warfare of Science with Theology in Christendom*

SCIENCE

❑ Jacob Bronowski—*The Identity of Man*
❑ Nicolaus Copernicus—*On the Revolutions of Heavenly Spheres*
❑ Francis Crick—*Of Molecules and Men*
❑ Marie Curie—*Radioactive Substances*
❑ Charles Darwin—*The Autobiography of Charles Darwin*
❑ Charles Darwin—*The Descent of Man*
❑ Charles Darwin—*The Origin of Species*
❑ Charles Darwin—*The Voyage of the* Beagle
❑ René Descartes—*Treatise of Man*
❑ Albert Einstein—*Relativity*
❑ Michael Faraday—*The Forces of Matter*
❑ Galileo Galilei—*Dialogues Concerning Two New Sciences*
❑ Francis Galton—*Hereditary Genius*
❑ Ernst Haeckel—*The Riddle of the Universe*
❑ William Harvey—*On the Motion of the Heart and Blood in Animals*
❑ Werner Heisenberg—*Physics and Philosophy: The Revolution in Modern Science*
❑ Fred Hoyle—*Of Men and Galaxies*
❑ Julian Huxley—*Evolutionary Humanism*
❑ Thomas H. Huxley—*Evolution and Ethics* and *Science and Morals*
❑ Edward Jenner—*Vaccination against Smallpox*
❑ Johannes Kepler—*Epitome of Copernican Astronomy* and *Harmonies of the World*
❑ James Clerk Maxwell—*Matter and Motion*
❑ Isaac Newton—*Opticks, Or Treatise of the Reflections, Inflections, and Colours of Light*
❑ Isaac Newton—*The Principia*
❑ Louis Pasteur and Joseph Lister—*Germ Theory and Its Applications to Medicine* and *On the Antiseptic Principle of the Practice of Surgery*
❑ William Thomson (Lord Kelvin) and Peter Guthrie Tait—*The Elements of Natural Philosophy*
❑ Alfred Russel Wallace—*Island Life*

SOCIOLOGY

❑ Emile Durkheim—*Ethics and the Sociology of Morals*

GREAT BOOKS IN PHILOSOPHY PAPERBACK SERIES

ESTHETICS

❑ Aristotle—*The Poetics*
❑ Aristotle—*Treatise on Rhetoric*

ETHICS

❑ Aristotle—*The Nicomachean Ethics*
❑ Marcus Aurelius—*Meditations*
❑ Jeremy Bentham—*The Principles of Morals and Legislation*

- ❑ John Dewey—*Human Nature and Conduct*
- ❑ John Dewey—*The Moral Writings of John Dewey, Revised Edition*
- ❑ Epictetus—*Enchiridion*
- ❑ David Hume—*An Enquiry Concerning the Principles of Morals*
- ❑ Immanuel Kant—*Fundamental Principles of the Metaphysic of Morals*
- ❑ John Stuart Mill—*Utilitarianism*
- ❑ George Edward Moore—*Principia Ethica*
- ❑ Friedrich Nietzsche—*Beyond Good and Evil*
- ❑ Plato—*Protagoras, Philebus, and Gorgias*
- ❑ Bertrand Russell—*Bertrand Russell On Ethics, Sex, and Marriage*
- ❑ Arthur Schopenhauer—*The Wisdom of Life* and *Counsels and Maxims*
- ❑ Adam Smith—*The Theory of Moral Sentiments*
- ❑ Benedict de Spinoza—*Ethics* including
    The Improvement of the Understanding

LOGIC

- ❑ George Boole—*The Laws of Thought*

METAPHYSICS/EPISTEMOLOGY

- ❑ Aristotle—*De Anima*
- ❑ Aristotle—*The Metaphysics*
- ❑ Francis Bacon—*Essays*
- ❑ George Berkeley—*Three Dialogues Between Hylas and Philonous*
- ❑ W. K. Clifford—*The Ethics of Belief and Other Essays*
- ❑ René Descartes—*Discourse on Method* and *The Meditations*
- ❑ John Dewey—*How We Think*
- ❑ John Dewey—*The Influence of Darwin on Philosophy and Other Essays*
- ❑ Epicurus—*The Essential Epicurus: Letters, Principal Doctrines,*
    Vatican Sayings, and Fragments
- ❑ Sidney Hook—*The Quest for Being*
- ❑ David Hume—*An Enquiry Concerning Human Understanding*
- ❑ David Hume—*A Treatise on Human Nature*
- ❑ William James—*The Meaning of Truth*
- ❑ William James—*Pragmatism*
- ❑ Immanuel Kant—*The Critique of Judgment*
- ❑ Immanuel Kant—*Critique of Practical Reason*
- ❑ Immanuel Kant—*Critique of Pure Reason*
- ❑ Gottfried Wilhelm Leibniz—*Discourse on Metaphysics* and the *Monadology*
- ❑ John Locke—*An Essay Concerning Human Understanding*
- ❑ George Herbert Mead—*The Philosophy of the Present*
- ❑ Michel de Montaigne—*Essays*
- ❑ Charles S. Peirce—*The Essential Writings*
- ❑ Plato—*The Euthyphro, Apology, Crito, and Phaedo*
- ❑ Plato—*Lysis, Phaedrus, and Symposium*
- ❑ Bertrand Russell—*The Problems of Philosophy*
- ❑ George Santayana—*The Life of Reason*
- ❑ Arthur Schopenhauer—*On the Principle of Sufficient Reason*
- ❑ Sextus Empiricus—*Outlines of Pyrrhonism*
- ❑ Alfred North Whitehead—*The Concept of Nature*
- ❑ Ludwig Wittgenstein—*Wittgenstein's Lectures: Cambridge, 1932–1935*

PHILOSOPHY OF RELIGION

- ❏ Jeremy Bentham—*The Influence of Natural Religion on the Temporal Happiness of Mankind*
- ❏ Marcus Tullius Cicero—*The Nature of the Gods* and *On Divination*
- ❏ Ludwig Feuerbach—*The Essence of Christianity*
- ❏ Ludwig Feuerbach—*The Essence of Religion*
- ❏ Paul Henri Thiry, Baron d'Holbach—*Good Sense*
- ❏ David Hume—*Dialogues Concerning Natural Religion*
- ❏ William James—*The Varieties of Religious Experience*
- ❏ John Locke—*A Letter Concerning Toleration*
- ❏ Lucretius—*On the Nature of Things*
- ❏ John Stuart Mill—*Three Essays on Religion*
- ❏ Friedrich Nietzsche—*The Antichrist*
- ❏ Thomas Paine—*The Age of Reason*
- ❏ Bertrand Russell—*Bertrand Russell On God and Religion*

SOCIAL AND POLITICAL PHILOSOPHY

- ❏ Aristotle—*The Politics*
- ❏ Mikhail Bakunin—*The Basic Bakunin: Writings, 1869–1871*
- ❏ Edmund Burke—*Reflections on the Revolution in France*
- ❏ John Dewey—*Freedom and Culture*
- ❏ John Dewey—*Individualism Old and New*
- ❏ John Dewey—*Liberalism and Social Action*
- ❏ G. W. F. Hegel—*The Philosophy of History*
- ❏ G. W. F. Hegel—*Philosophy of Right*
- ❏ Thomas Hobbes—*The Leviathan*
- ❏ Sidney Hook—*Paradoxes of Freedom*
- ❏ Sidney Hook—*Reason, Social Myths, and Democracy*
- ❏ John Locke—*The Second Treatise on Civil Government*
- ❏ Niccolo Machiavelli—*The Prince*
- ❏ Karl Marx (with Friedrich Engels)—*The German Ideology*, including *Theses on Feuerbach* and *Introduction to the Critique of Political Economy*
- ❏ Karl Marx—*The Poverty of Philosophy*
- ❏ Karl Marx/Friedrich Engels—*The Economic and Philosophic Manuscripts of 1844* and *The Communist Manifesto*
- ❏ John Stuart Mill—*Considerations on Representative Government*
- ❏ John Stuart Mill—*On Liberty*
- ❏ John Stuart Mill—*On Socialism*
- ❏ John Stuart Mill—*The Subjection of Women*
- ❏ Montesquieu, Charles de Secondat—*The Spirit of Laws*
- ❏ Friedrich Nietzsche—*Thus Spake Zarathustra*
- ❏ Thomas Paine—*Common Sense*
- ❏ Thomas Paine—*Rights of Man*
- ❏ Plato—*Laws*
- ❏ Plato—*The Republic*
- ❏ Jean-Jacques Rousseau—*Émile*
- ❏ Jean-Jacques Rousseau—*The Social Contract*
- ❏ Bertrand Russell—*Political Ideals*
- ❏ Mary Wollstonecraft—*A Vindication of the Rights of Men*
- ❏ Mary Wollstonecraft—*A Vindication of the Rights of Women*

NOTES

NOTES

NOTES

NOTES

NOTES

NOTES